FORTY-DEUCE

Alan Bowne

BROADWAY PLAY PUBLISHING INC
New York
www.broadwayplaypublishing.com
info@broadwayplaypublishing.com

FORTY-DEUCE
© Copyright 1997 Alan Bowne

All rights reserved. This work is fully protected under the copyright laws of the United States of America. No part of this publication may be photocopied, reproduced, stored in a retrieval system, or transmitted, in any form or by any means, electronic, mechanical, recording, or otherwise, without the prior permission of the publisher. Additional copies of this play are available from the publisher.

Written permission is required for live performance of any sort. This includes readings, cuttings, scenes, and excerpts. For amateur and stock performances, please contact Broadway Play Publishing Inc. For all other rights contact the author c/o B P P I.

First published by B P P I in *Plays By Alan Bowne* in 1997
This edition: July 2016
I S B N: 978-0-88145-675-2
Book design: Marie Donovan
Page make-up: Adobe InDesign
Typeface: Palatino
Printed and bound in the U S A

FORTY-DEUCE opened in workshop at the Perry Street Theater in New York City on 20 February 1981. It was produced by Steven Steinlauf, with the following cast and creative contributor:

AUGIE	John Seitz
MITCHELL	Thomas Waites
RICKY	Barry Miller
CRANK	Willie Reale
BLOW	John Pankow
JOHN ANTHONY	Timothy Mathias
ROPER	William Hunt
Director	Sheldon Larry

FORTY-DEUCE reopened at the same theater on 11 October 1981. It was produced by Steven Steinlauf and Anne Thomson, with the following cast and creative contributor:

AUGIE	Harris Laskawy
MITCHELL	Ahvi Spindell
RICKY	Kevin Bacon
CRANK	Tommy Citera
BLOW	Mark Keyloun
JOHN ANTHONY	John Noonan
ROPER	Orson Bean
Director	Tony Tanner

The author wishes to thank Michael Cristofer for his invaluable assistance in editing the script.

CHARACTERS & SETTING

AUGIE, *Brooklyn Italian, in his forties*
MITCHELL, *Manhattan Jewish, in his late teens*
RICKY, *Brooklyn Italian, in his late teens*
CRANK, *Brooklyn Italian, in his late teens*
BLOW, *Lower East Side Ukrainian, in his late teens*
JOHN ANTHONY, *WASP, in his early teens*
ROPER, *WASP, about fifty years old*

Time: The present

Setting: The environs of Times Square, a Sunday in the middle of a suffocating August in New York City

A single set: a dingy room overlooking Eighth Avenue. A few sticks of battered furniture—chairs, a table—including, against the back wall, a bureau with peeling mirror. A disproportionately large unmade bed, possibly tilted downstage, so that a nude body, curved and twisted upon it, is made the visual focus throughout. It is a conventional hotel room, with entrance door, bathroom door, and window, its aged crinkled shade half drawn.

Note: The dialogue's orthography and punctuation, if occasionally unorthodox, is deliberate. A glossary is provided at the end of the play.

For John Paul Hudson and Ed Kruse

"...these torture rooms of the living idiom."

ACT ONE

Scene One

(The curtain rises on JOHN ANTHONY, *nude on the bed, his slender form twisted in sleep.)*

(The murky yellow light of a hot New York City summer afternoon glows through the open window. There are the occasional rumble of the subway and low traffic sounds throughout.)

(Out of the open bathroom doorway there sticks a naked human foot, big, broad, and dirty, twitching on the floor.)

(Enter AUGIE *through the entrance door, after we hear a rasping of keys in the automatic lock. He pauses by the bed and stares at the boy asleep upon it.)*

AUGIE: Jeez. Fuckin' jeez.

*(*AUGIE *bends over the bed, peering more intently at* JOHN ANTHONY, *who remains sleeping.)*

AUGIE: Up the fuckin' ass. Off the wall and up the fuckin' ass.

*(*AUGIE *shakes* JOHN ANTHONY. *The boy does not wake.)*

AUGIE: You better not be for Chrissakes dead. Hey, fuck nuts, I'm talking to you.

(The foot sticking from the open bathroom doorway twitches violently. Slowly MITCHELL *sits up and leans out.)*

MITCHELL: Augie? God, Augie, she's shitface.

AUGIE: *(To* MITCHELL*)* How's from this twerp?

MITCHELL: *(Referring to himself)* Shitface I tell you. Been to breakfast with a shrankroid? *(He starts crawling towards* AUGIE.*)*

AUGIE: Did I ask you a question, bitch?

MITCHELL: We was holin' some shit, me and Crank and Ricky? Some shit you would never know it was dope.

(AUGIE *crosses to a chair by the window, stepping over* MITCHELL. AUGIE *sits, his legs spread, hands dangling ominously between them.)*

AUGIE: Did I fuckin' ask you a fuckin' question you cock suck you mother suck?

*(*MITCHELL *has crawled to the bed. He raises himself to sit on the bed's margin.)*

MITCHELL: You know how sometimes when it's good you rush like... *(His hands rise in a geiser motion.)* Wooooooooooosh: *puff! (On the last syllable, his fingertips delicately explode.)* Well, this was like.... *(The geiser motion again)* Wooooooooooosh: *blat! (On last syllable, he makes a loud, flatulent noise.)*

AUGIE: The twerp. On the bed.

MITCHELL: Oh sure. Her too. Ricky snatched her off a Greyhound. *(He looks around, under bed.)* Purse's here somewhere. Got a cigarette?

AUGIE: Fuckin' bozo queen bozo fuck.

(He stands abruptly up. MITCHELL *reacts.* AUGIE *crosses to window.)*

AUGIE: That guinea testicle I leave in charge? *(He sends window shade flapping up. Looks out)* Creepy fuckin' steambath Eighth Avenue at... *(Looks at watch)* At three-thirty Sunday afternoon. Up the fuckin' ass out the window on the fuckin' street. Jeez.

ACT ONE

(MITCHELL *locates his bag under bed. Removes a brush from it, crosses to bureau.*)

MITCHELL: You should of been here Saturday night. *(He looks into mirror. Begins brushing hair.)* I seen this dogfight. A coupla German Shepherds belong to these two blind spades workin' the same corner? *(He begins goofing into the mirror.)* "Watch yo' ass, nigger, this here *my* turf." "Let the *dogs* decide, sucker." And those Shepherds, Augie, they was cock- suckin' two of the *nastiest* girls on Forty-deuce. I *mean*? Usually dogs got the big watery eyes go, you know, "twenny-five cents, thirty-five cents, make it fifty"? Shit, they rip out your pussy. Such a scene. And nobody, you know? Nobody give a ka-fuck. Twenny million niggers and spics, ten million dope fiends, forty truckloads of faggots from New Jersey, two hunnert thousand hookers and six stupid cops. Augie. Listen. I need a vacation. It's hard on a Jewish queen. *(Goofing again.)* "Wanna fuck?" "Wanna get high?" "Wanna suck fuck toke poke peel feel and get *numb*?" Dope and sex and dope and sex and dope. Augie, you come up with the third kick I marry you?

AUGIE: You come up with Ricky I break your arm.

(MITCHELL *ceases brushing hair.*)

MITCHELL: O K. I think he's in the bat'room. *(Pause)* Asleep on the toilet?

(AUGIE *continues gazing out the window.*)

AUGIE: *(Toneless.)* Asleep on the toilet.

MITCHELL: He passes out on the toilet. I pass out on the bat'room floor. The kid drags it in here, passes out on the bed. Crank don't bat a cocksuckin' eyelash, he just asks which way is the door, and dances.

AUGIE: *(Toneless)* Asleep on the fuckin' toilet.

(MITCHELL *crosses to bed, rummages under it, pulls out a pair of high heels.*)

MITCHELL: Augie. Don't worry. Money? He's *got* money.

AUGIE: Those new ones I send up here?

(MITCHELL *is putting on the high heels.*)

MITCHELL: Those rabbis? Jesus, Augie. Plus, I turned one from the Haymarket, but that's mine.

(AUGIE *turns from window to face* MITCHELL.)

AUGIE: You use this room?

MITCHELL: Sure I use this room. I give Ricky a cut for this room.

AUGIE: You use this room one of your tricks you deal with me.

MITCHELL: And where was you?

AUGIE: None of your asshole. You deal with me or you go fuck all. There's this, and the place on Forty-sixth, and the room across Port Authority. You wanna use the facilities you don't deal with nobody but me.

MITCHELL: I deal with you since I'm on the street.

(AUGIE *stares at* MITCHELL *in silence, then moves from the window to stare into the offstage bathroom. Enters bathroom. A slapping sound can be heard.* MITCHELL *winces with each slap.*)

MITCHELL: *(Continued)* Ka-fuck.

(AUGIE *marches a bleary* RICKY *out of bathroom. Brings him downstage center; and tries to stand him up.* RICKY *keeps slumping against* AUGIE, *who slaps the youth's face.*)

AUGIE: The money, you little shit. I send two new ones up here.

RICKY: *(Thickly)* What you fuck?

ACT ONE 5

AUGIE: And you put a twelve-year-old to work in my room. You tank up a twelve-year-old put him to work in my facilities.

RICKY: What you fuck?

(RICKY *tries to back away from* AUGIE, *who slaps him.*)

AUGIE: Sixteen, that's O K, sixteen, I can handle sixteen. *(Slaps* RICKY's *face)*

AUGIE: Even maybe say fifteen, I can handle fifteen. *(Slaps* RICKY *again)*

AUGIE: But how I explain to Mike about twelve? Hey? How I explain this here twelve-year-old to Mike? This ain't no agency operation, you testicle. This here is bang-and-walk.

(RICKY *slides to the floor.*)

AUGIE: You can't work no twelve-year-old outa rooms on the Square. What you think, you workin' for some white man does business over the phone outa some floorthrough Upper East with the Bloomingdale's pillows and rugs and shit? You a greasy little guinea and you workin' for a greaser and I know the rules this fuckin' neighborhood and I say I don't handle no twelve-year-old fags!

(AUGIE *jerks* RICKY's *head up by his hair.*)

AUGIE: Unnerstand?

MITCHELL: Augie. Hey. Listen. I think the message is definitely getting through?

(AUGIE *releases* RICKY *and crosses to bed to stand in front of* MITCHELL, *whom he fixes with his finger.*)

AUGIE: You. You wrap up that chickie. You take her over to G G's you tell her to work outa there. What they do in that armpit is their business prob'ly give her a fuckin' trophy or somethin'. Whole lotta street twats dressed up for Christmas anyhow. *(He turns, stares at floor.)* Twelve-year-old hustler bring Mike up my pussy so fuckin' fast I get hemmeroids. *(He crosses to* RICKY *and bends over him.)* Clean up the Square that's what they oughta do, you greaseball. You member what went down all them niggers runnin' the twelve-year-old white chicks? Well, that ain't gonna happen my facilities no fuckin' way. *(He moves to the chair, sits, his hands dangling between his legs. Vaguely addresses room.)* I lose my protection you bitches have to suck it off in the street. Mike blacklist you every hotel in the Square. *(He begins nodding his head.)* This here is clean, it's quick, and it's guaranteed. *(Pause)* This here is like a Burger King.

(RICKY *begins to retch.* MITCHELL *crosses to him.)*

MITCHELL: We didn't oughta hole that ka-fuckin' motor oil. *(Strokes* RICKY's *head)* Don't you feel shittier'n shit? *(Addresses* AUGIE*)* You want I should get some coffee that bodega downstairs?

AUGIE: *(To* RICKY*)* The money, greaseball.

MITCHELL: *(To* RICKY*)* Hey. The man wants the rent. Let's put you on the bed. That's right. Up we go.

(MITCHELL *helps* RICKY *to his feet and crosses with him to the bed.* RICKY *sits on the bed's right margin.)*

MITCHELL: Hey. You want I should get us some coffee? Ricky? *(Addresses* JOHN ANTHONY's *slumbering body)* Hey. Move over.

(MITCHELL *shakes* JOHN ANTHONY, *who stirs, comes to stupefied life, sits up, looks about wild and unseeing, and rolls over to lie on his stomach.)*

RICKY: *(Thickly)* Buncha twenny dollar tricks up your ass twenny dollar tricks.

AUGIE: You don't like the action you can fuck off—go back East New York. Know what I mean?

ACT ONE

RICKY: I got a deal goin' you look cheap standing next to it.

AUGIE: You owe me, greaseball. You owe me from last night. You fuckin' owe me from two weeks ago.

RICKY: These two niggers, one is a dyke. She has a whole lotta blow. This one's buying into it.

AUGIE: So?

RICKY: This one's investing.

AUGIE: So?

RICKY: This one is copping.

AUGIE: So?

RICKY: So I taste it. So it's uncut. So I pay you back.

AUGIE: You owe me, greaseball. I put you in charge, you fuck up.

RICKY: I turn those two yids you send up here. That your idea of trade—two fuckin' bearded yids?

MITCHELL: They was *weird*, Augie. Like straight outa *shul*. I thought they was gonna pray over us.

AUGIE: *(To* RICKY*)* Kike money, nigger money, what you fuckin' care?

RICKY: Tried to get away with fifteen. You tell them fifteen, you fuck.

AUGIE: So you service both at once. That's thirty.

RICKY: My asshole.

(There is banging at the door. MITCHELL *moves to entrance door and admits* CRANK.*)*

CRANK: Mitchell? Was that shit shit?

MITCHELL: Could'a died, you syphilis.

CRANK: Hey. Augie.

AUGIE: Crank. Money.

CRANK: Ricky and me we got this operation we pay you later? Hey. Ricky. *(He approaches bed; looks down at* RICKY.*)*

AUGIE: *(To* CRANK*)* I own these facilities. I fuckin' own *you* from last week. Any tricks get turned, any dope trade hands, I get my commission. Ricky tells me he such a testicle he deal with some jig dyke got fancy stuff. You the other testicle?

CRANK: *(To* RICKY*)* Some mother shit, wadn't it? Augie. There's this dyke—her old man? Says he'll front us. Last night we party? Only I use this shit offa Blow.

MITCHELL: Crank, you want I should go get some coffee?

RICKY: Five C's, Augie. All we need is five C's. The niggers front us the rest.

CRANK: I can cut it, carry it, like in two hours?

AUGIE: Where these niggers get this blow?

CRANK: Fuck if I know. But the mothers is close, Augie. Real close. Only they gotta move fast. By tonight.

AUGIE: Why some niggers front you fuck? Two goddamn queers.

RICKY: *(To* CRANK*)* You listen to her? Every hooker use this room she say push the milk sugar. Every East Side bitch every New Jersey twat every cheap Toyota cruisin' Third Avenue. She knows faggots snort coke like...

MITCHELL: Like it was gonna make their cocks grow.

CRANK: 'Cept for them schmucks last night? Jesus. The fuzzy one in the dumb hat? He don't even take it off.

RICKY: Augie's the fuckin' Jew. He don't want no competition. Crappy milk sugar act all excited so suckin' cheap.

ACT ONE 9

AUGIE: *(To* RICKY*)* You commission me, you nigger. Mike don't go for no independent action.

RICKY: Mike don't have to know.

AUGIE: Where a little greaser like you get a slice of any kind of anything?

RICKY: That midtown three-piece with the silver wig? He pay plenty for that fetus. *(He jerks his thumb at* JOHN ANTHONY, *behind him.)*

*(*AUGIE *abruptly rises.)*

AUGIE: You mean Roper? You goin' for Roper? You nose into my contacts I cut it off. I stuff it up your big flappin' asshole.

RICKY: Too late. He's innerested.

AUGIE: Roper is very upper class, Ricky. Very...upper... class.

MITCHELL: I know that number. Weird? Blow and me once we see him comm outa Sixth Avenue. You ready for this? *(Gestures)* Blow cocksuckin' waves.

CRANK: And the john fuckin' waves back, right?

*(*AUGIE *is still on his feet, staring at* RICKY.*)*

AUGIE: Roper's Mike's special. Likes a production. *(Points at* RICKY.*)* Mike burn your ass he find out. *(He sits abruptly down; hands fidget between his legs.)* Copping Mike's special. Jeez. Fuckin' jeez.

RICKY: Mike ain't gonna know. Augie, think with your fuckin' head. Some little creep like third rate numbers runner like cheapo bagman sittin on *your* face. We gotta open this up or we gonna get old and yellow you and me and Crank like the stains on these sheets. *(He stands; crosses to* AUGIE.*)* Roper don't care fuck. He play, you bring the ball. That little kid is a goddam virgin. Stone him he'll do anything won't know from shit.

AUGIE: Jeez.

(CRANK *reaches across bed; shakes* JOHN ANTHONY.)

CRANK: Hey. John Anthony.

MITCHELL: *(To* CRANK*)* She stinks, don't she?

CRANK: How the fuck I know she stink?

MITCHELL: Long bus ride from ka-fucking nowhere.

(JOHN ANTHONY *jerks suddenly to life, sits up, stares with great eyes ringed, unseeing, burning, straight at audience. Then he plops sideways and curls into a ball in the middle of the bed.)*

RICKY: *(To* AUGIE.*)* Roper he comes by later. All hotted up and cash in his pants.

AUGIE: Fuckin' jeez.

(RICKY *suddenly grips his belly; returns to bed, sitting next to* CRANK.*)*

RICKY: What was *in* that shit?

MITCHELL: *(Generally)* Want I should go get some coffee?

CRANK: So Mitchell. Ditn't you turn one last night?

MITCHELL: I give a dime to Blow, I shoot last night's on three cards.

CRANK: Three cards?

MITCHELL: Red black black red. This dealer he had his old lady along and are you ready? She hadda kid in this baby carriage standin' right next to the Monte table. I could vomit it was so cheap. Fucks your timing all to fuck. You thinkin', I win and I take the Gerbers from this black brat. Now is that cheap?

CRANK: Woulda fucked *my* timing, Mitchell.

ACT ONE 11

AUGIE: *(To* RICKY*)* O K, greaseball. Get this. Thirty percent. By tomorrow morning not a speck of nigger coke in these facilities.

CRANK: Thirty! That leaves...that leaves what?

RICKY: Enough. *(To* AUGIE*)* O K, you fuckin' bloodsucker.

AUGIE: Mike find out, I'm dead. So what does that mean, bloodsucker?

MITCHELL: That bodega downstairs. Four coffees. Regular? Xtra light? Light?

(AUGIE *rummages for change.*)

AUGIE: Fuck them spics. Go to the corner Forty-fifth. The Greeks.

MITCHELL: They charge twice as much the Greeks.

(RICKY *is in evident pain, his head bowed.*)

RICKY: Money suckin' Greek bastards everywhere you look. Charge you a dollar for a glass of water. *(To* MITCHELL*)* Carton of milk.

(AUGIE *gives money to* MITCHELL.*)*

AUGIE: The Greeks. Xtra light. Take Ricky's keys.

RICKY: A carton of milk. The bodega. Crank. Give her the money.

(CRANK *draws crumpled bills from jeans; hands to* MITCHELL.*)*

CRANK: The bodega.

MITCHELL: What am I, gonna go downstairs for you corner Forty-fifth for Augie? What am I?

(RICKY *begins speaking in gasps, head bowed.*)

RICKY: Fuckin' Greeks eighty-five cents for a Diet-Rite four dollars for a lousy pancake. Fuckin' Greeks fuckin' mothers. They come over here make a few bucks offa hot cigarettes souvlaki sandwiches. Buy up every shit corner this town. You can't get a fuckin' cup of coffee 'tween Forty-two and Fifty, Eight over to Five, some Greek don't charge you up the rectum. Orange juice? A lousy pint of orange juice the Greeks make you drop your pants. Push out all the bodegas shoot up the prices take over the Square. Screw the numbers people, the peddlers, the loose joints, the hookers, charge us up the pee-hole pack pieces under their big fat cash register smiles you walk in. Send the fuckers back to Astoria piss on their two by four lawns.

AUGIE: O K, O K. The bodega.

MITCHELL: That's big of you, Augie, know what I mean?

AUGIE: The coffee, you yo-yo.

MITCHELL: Xtra light! Crank, you want light? Ricky, a carton of milk. What about the kid?

RICKY: Milk for him too. A toasted corn. Or a bran, toasted, with orange marmalade.

MITCHELL: Orange marmalade?

RICKY: Or a English.

AUGIE: A glass'a egg cream. Take the edge off the breath 'tween her legs.

MITCHELL: And bring down her price? *(Exits through entrance door after snatching* RICKY's *keys)*

AUGIE: *(To* RICKY*)* Thirty plus my commission last night. Two at fifteen—one at twenny.

RICKY: What fuckin' one at twenny?

AUGIE: *(Meaning* MITCHELL*)* That Jew bitch turn one these facilities. That's all mine. I leave you in charge it's just a fuckin' favor. Jeez. Give him a piece greaseball thinks it's Christmas. Thinks he's runnin' things. Dumb

ACT ONE 13

little guinea with the big head. *(Deliberately)* Guinea fuck up I got no choice.

RICKY: It's in the pocket.

(There is a quick tapping at the door. CRANK *crosses to door and admits* BLOW, *a package under his arm.)*

BLOW: *(To* CRANK*)* Hey. I just see Mitchell? I get eat out by this Long Island—tells me about his wife. Augie. Where was you last night? Asshole looks Wall Street his shoes to his dyed hair. Wears these forty dollar faded jeans. Wants me to talk dirty? For him the Dixie Hotel is slumming. His underwear is bleached? Sniffs my pits and makes a face. Fuck I wash this morning.

AUGIE: *(To* BLOW*)* We got three testicles this fuckin' deal?

BLOW: What fuckin' three? What deal?

RICKY: *(To* BLOW*)* You poison me, you shit.

CRANK: Blow, you poison Ricky.

BLOW: *(To* RICKY*)* Hey. You geeze that scum? I ditn't know you geeze that scum.

CRANK: What else?

BLOW: I front you that scum.

AUGIE: You a third testicle, Blow? The niggers all this fancy-ass coke?

BLOW: I don't know from Ricky's deals. I don't work for you, Augie.

AUGIE: *(Toneless)* You don't work for me.

BLOW: Maybe I turn a trick here. Maybe you get a piece of that. But I don't hang out here, Augie.

AUGIE: Blow, you don't work for me, you don't work for nobody, right?

BLOW: I sell dick I sell dope. I come I go.

AUGIE: You come you go. I don't own your asshole, right? So why is your fuckin' asshole in my facilities?

BLOW: Augie. Last night I drop off some shit. It's discount, know what I mean? You wanna piece of that? Ricky say fuck yes he can handle it. So I front him. Only the dumb shit pokes it up his arm.

RICKY: You front me my fuckin' ass. Scrape it outa pussy some Ninth Avenue transie.

BLOW: So how's the kid?

RICKY: So what's the kid to you?

BLOW: I talk to that kid last night. Told him, hey, I bring you a present.

RICKY: That kid don't need presents from no fuckin' bohunk. That kid is my business.

BLOW: Hey. You watch it with him?

RICKY: What you fuck?

BLOW: He don't get hurt. Easy up?

CRANK: Ricky say, Roper's the one.

BLOW: Roper.

CRANK: We got plans?

BLOW: Crank, you crazy you throw that kid at Roper. I know Roper. I do Roper. He's fuckin' Upper East.

CRANK: We got plans. Ricky?

RICKY: I go into the bat'room. I put my face in a sink of water. I come out. There is nobody's bohunk nose in my business. *(He rises painfully, crosses to bathroom, enters and slams the door.)*

AUGIE: *(Loudly)* That was O K. I mean he's sick and all but that was O K. *(Normal voice)* Hot shit greaser.

CRANK: *(To* BLOW*)* You really buy him a present?

(BLOW *ignores* CRANK *and crosses to bed.*)

ACT ONE 15

BLOW: Hey. John Anthony. *(He kneels on bed.)* Look what I brung you. *(He undoes package.)* You said, you saw this T-shirt? I said, but it's tacky? You said, yeah, but you was gonna buy it. *(He shows the T-shirt; it has the words "New York City" and an apple printed on it.)* I got it small cause you so fuckin' little.

CRANK: *(To* AUGIE*)* Ricky and me, it's a hunnert percent sure thing?

AUGIE: Testicle.

CRANK: It works, and then we got a operation?

AUGIE: Not in my facilities. This a one-shot on account Mike can't know. I shouldn't taken off last night.

BLOW: *(To* JOHN ANTHONY.*)* Like I was sayin' before, maybe we team up. I take you over to the Haymarket, introduce you? Gotta hang out somewhere. *(He lowers his voice.)* This a rip, kid.

CRANK: Hey. Maybe we deal with Mike?

AUGIE: Testicle. You deal with me you deal with Mike.

CRANK: O.K. We deal with you we deal with Mike.

BLOW: Hey. I brung you this tacky bullshit shirt. *(He lowers his voice.)* Come on, kid. Wake the fuck up.

AUGIE: I get this operation by fuckin' with Mike's specials? Mike you know where Mike is comin' from? You save me trouble, I cut you in. You make me trouble, I cut you out. Eight, ten operations he got to have managers. Run here run fuck. He got no time. And time, you testicle, that is the reason for everything.

BLOW: *(Low tones)* I come back for you later? *(He begins stroking* JOHN ANTHONY's *hair.)*

CRANK: Time? Augie?

AUGIE: Time means I can do this and that and fuck it I move free don't answer to nobody. So what you got the

East Sixties floorthrough and a condo in the Hamptons! You got to do this for that one and see her and bend over for this one and suck the other one's hole. You maybe get paid good but you still a fuckin' whore. You take Roper.

BLOW: *(To* CRANK*)* Hey. Is the kid sick?

CRANK: We all sick that slime you feed us.

BLOW: *(Jerking round)* You shoot him with that?

CRANK: I shoot the room, I shoot myself. Augie?

AUGIE: Consultant she calls herself. Oil companies. Plastics. Big cocksuckin' deal. Anyhow she sittin' hunnerth floor Sixth Avenue with a big ugly bone on. Or they fuckin' send her to Houston where she can't even cross her fuckin' legs. She tell me once, in New York they deliver the goods. Bitch goes to Paris, to It'ly, to fuckin' Africa. She say, only New York. In New York, she say, kicks? They let you run up a tab, bill you quarterly. Saves you time. On the mother *street*. Tell *her* about time.

BLOW: *(Low tones)* Don't never do no shit these here numbers, know what I mean?

AUGIE: With guys like Roper you gotta know the fuck you doin. You don't say, hey. I got this twelve-year-old stashed up Eighth Avenue. Fresh off the suckin' bus. Sure she show up lickin her lips. Cause she know she dealin' with amateurs. It could be dangerous. It fires her ass. But something go wrong she don't complain to you. She go to Mike. She can't come. Hey? Or the kid he get hurt. Or she gets her tits in a wringer. Or maybe some undercover cocksuck has add it up for hisself follow her up here. The bitch get scared Mike gotta fix. Then where you are? Testicle! People keep trippin' over this big smelly fat kid dead in the street.

ACT ONE

BLOW: *(Low tones)* Bastards. Would I put a spike through that skin?

(RICKY *emerges from the bathroom towelling his face. He glares at the two on the bed.)*

CRANK: Hey. Ricky. We got a operation?

RICKY: *(Eyes on bed)* What else?

AUGIE: Dumb ass greaser. I got this operation fuckin' with Mike?

RICKY: *(Eyes on bed)* This turkey room is no operation.

(On the bed, BLOW *begins tentatively stroking* JOHN ANTHONY's *body.)*

AUGIE: Mike now he knows. Got his fingers up bitches like Roper. Did Mike ever give out with the real fuckin' thing? Tank up some slut offa Fifty-third maybe. Say she such a virgin you could eat outa her jockstrap hand her to Roper does *that* bitch know or fuckin' care? Bitches like Roper they come Forty-deuce offa fucking Madison Ave, offa fuckin' Lex. They think the shit on the floor is outa some movie. Like them Roper bitches is innocent, you nigger. They used to pickin' up phones and pressin' buttons. They order outa some catalog. Hooker flops out with the rubber-plated tits flashbulbs 'tween his legs disco music screamin' out his asshole. Control. You got to control every shit detail you deal with guys like that.

RICKY: *(Eyes on bed)* Every cheap shot this town scared somebody gonna grab a little.

(BLOW *stiffens suddenly on the bed.)*

BLOW: Hey.

AUGIE: Down to the minute. Guys like that they fuckin' cream on a schedule so tight you better be sure nothin' interfere. Control, you greaser. Control.

RICKY: *(To* BLOW*)* What you fuck?

BLOW: He's cacked.

(RICKY *crosses at once to the bed. Pushes* BLOW *to one side and bends over* JOHN ANTHONY, *feeling for his pulse.*)

BLOW: Is this for real? Cacked?

(*Enter* MITCHELL, *with paper bag, through door after rasping of lock.*)

MITCHELL: Coffee wagon! So will you line up, girls? (*He begins taking each item out of sack and placing it on bureau.*)

(RICKY *drops* JOHN ANTHONY's *wrist and covers his mouth with his hand. Everyone except* MITCHELL *is frozen.*)

MITCHELL: Xtra light for Augie? Regular is for me, and does she need this danish? Light for Crank. Ricky? Carton of milk. Nothing for you, Blow, you eat my dime you suck dick. A toasted corn, Ricky. No bran. And marmalade I ask you does a P R know from marmalade? I go, Hey mon. Lay a little grape jelly on the dried-up thing. He looks at me. I go, So mash up a fuckin' fried banana or something don't leave it all crusty like a goddamned scab? He looks at me. I go, Besides two boxes Uncle Ben's white rice, a can of peaches, seven Hershey bars and cigarettes, what the fuck you got in this store? (*Pause*) You know?

(*No one responds.* AUGIE *crosses quickly to bed, slips his hand under the boy's chest, stares wildly, then sinks to bed's margin, head in hands.*)

AUGIE: Fuckin' jeez.

MITCHELL: (*Looking from one to the other.*) Hey. You want I should go back? (*Pause*) Ricky? (*Pause. He uses his fingers to itemize.*) Xtra light. (*Pause*) Light. (*Pause*) A carton of fuckin' milk. (*Pause*) And a toasted corn. (*Pause*) Hey. Does a P R know from marmalade?

(*Silence. Lights down.*)

ACT ONE

Scene Two

(A short while later. MITCHELL's *consignment of plastic cups is scattered now about the floor; as aimlessly as the characters themselves.)*

(A sheet has been hastily thrown over JOHN ANTHONY's *body, but his feet and an outstretched arm, fingers curled, are still visible.)*

(The window shade is fully drawn now, but AUGIE *has turned back an edge and is peering down into the street. He is ominously silent.* RICKY *sits backwards in a chair, looking at* AUGIE. CRANK *squats on the floor between them, glancing furtively from one to the other.* BLOW *sits on the bed's left margin, staring at the wall.* MITCHELL *is half-supine on the floor; propped against the bed's foot, his long legs, capped in heels, thrown out before him. He is meditatively munching a danish.)*

MITCHELL: Hey. Maybe we set fire to this fuckin' building? Who would know from just another body all burn to a crisp? Just last week right on Forty-two. Hey Blow you was there.

*(*BLOW *does not respond.)*

MITCHELL: All them hookers in the massage parlor hangin out the third story. Everybody on the street yellin Fire, ya dumb bitches! The whole top three floors is on fuckin' fire. Girls so stoned they start carrying on you know hangin' out the windows with the wigs and the tits figure the fire is good for business? So who woulda know coupla girls check out in that one you think anybody ask questions? *(Pause)* Hey. The only time I see a dead body was my grandmother? Such a drunk my grandmother. I never see her since I'm like fifteen? For a Jew my old man was not family-orientated. We live East Side, my grandmother was way the fuck on Staten Island? Coulda been Florida

all my dad care. Only time I'm on Staten Island was
the bitch's funeral. Ka-fuck. My dad. *(Pause)* Italian
neighborhood. Italians are very into funerals. Very
family-orientated. Hey. Crank's Italian. Crank. Italians
you know what I mean?

(CRANK *does not respond.*)

MITCHELL: There was this whole building Sixty-second
and First—practically give birth to our building Sixty-
fifth and Second? All the old grandmothers—big deal
every Sunday. Guineas and Jews and spics are up the
ka-pussy with family. Only my people, even when I
got a grandmother she lives way the fuck on Staten
Island? *(Pause)* It wadn't easy a big Jewish queen
Italian neighborhood. Coulda been worse, I know.
Coulda been Boro Park. *(Pause)* But I was a hitter.
(Pause) Anglo neighborhoods black neighborhoods
now they don't care so fuckin' much. Anglo guys my
neighborhood was goin' to college you know what
I mean? Some queen was just local color. But you
watch it with guineas. I don't even trust a faggot if he's
Italian. Or Spanish? Ricky will tell you these Italians.
Hey. Ricky.

(RICKY *does not respond.*)

MITCHELL: My ka-fucking dad. I wear these hot pants
once for the big fag crusade up Christopher every
year? Pink hot pants ride up my thighs you could see
my balls. Said I jiggled like the fringe on a chenille
bedspread. You think he give a shit? All the time
tanked to the tits, he just hope I ain't givin' no blow
jobs to no shvartzers? Ditn't want his kid goin' down
on no shvartzers. Only the goyim he says. He says, all
that pink skin and clean hair how could they give you
disease? My dad. *(Pause)* But you know sometimes I
think goyim are the worst. You take a spic—now O K
maybe he get mean. But if he got a bone on he fuck you

ACT ONE 21

up the ass, call it pussy, what the hell? But goyim they just look at you like you wadn't there or like the street was a movie and you was this extra? *(Pause)* But my dad—

AUGIE: *(Exploding)* Fuck your fuckin' dad! *(Finger rigidly extended, he turns to confront* RICKY.*)* So guinea you got it figured yet? You know what it cost move that dead cunt some place make it look like a accident? Know who you gotta deal with? The one them two niggers is comin' here to rip. The one what owns Roper's business. I say, hey Mike there this dead chicken in the Eighth Avenue apartment? With two niggers sellin' non-regulation shit to this uppity little greaser? What has his thumb up the twat one of your superspecial customers. So, Mike, hey. Can you fix it for me? *(Pause)* So, fuck nuts. You got it figured yet?

RICKY: I send Crank to tell the niggers.

AUGIE: Oh yeah right. And they go, Oh yeah sure that's O K we catch you next week.

RICKY: Only to come later. The deal is bigger now.

AUGIE: What?

RICKY: To come later. It take awhile now with Roper.

AUGIE: Yeah it take like the rest of your fuckin' life. Mike just make a phone call and greaser here can tell it to the Mid-town Precinct. They get here just in time to catch your act. *(He strides to bed, throws back the sheet.)* So what am I bid for this chicken. Hey? Here this stupid greaser queer tryin' to sell this skinny corpse to some uptown number who maybe can't tell when the trade is alive but who fuckin' knows a dead whore when he sees one. *(He begins furiously turning the body about.)* So what am I bid? Here's a foot fulla five stiff toes. Fifty cents. Here's a vein got a track so big you could run your cock half way up her arm. Dollar fifty?

Do I hear two? Ever see a mouth like that give you a blow job for days. Asshole tight as a drum butt like a rubber pad stick clamps on it. Scissor off her nipples wire her up and make her move. Wire her hands to her ankles her knee to her neck and her cock to her belly her foot to her mouth her neck bent back jerk and jiggle when you spread her legs—

(BLOW *turns, reaches across bed and grips* AUGIE's *wrist.*)

BLOW: That is a fuckin' dead body!

(AUGIE *stares at* BLOW.)

BLOW: There is a dead kid here?

(Pause)

AUGIE: Let go my arm you bohunk, you testicle.

(BLOW *releases* AUGIE.)

AUGIE: And leave us not forget who killed this fetus. This fetus was caved in by a lotta poison dope offa this twenny-five cent Uke called Blow.

(BLOW *turns and sinks onto bed again.* AUGIE *throws sheet carelessly over body and returns to window. He peers out.*)

AUGIE: What the fuck you mean, tell the niggers later?

RICKY: You can kill my ass, or Mike can kill my ass, what else can I do but use the kid if he's cacked or he's not? I got two ugly niggers kill my ass you don't. I gotta make that deal and that kid is my only way. Roper pay plenty he think he kill that kid. I tell you five Cs? Roper pay fuckin' five Gs he think he kill the kid. We tell the niggers, come later. They'll bite—for five fat ones.

AUGIE: *(Peering out window)* Big head on a little greaser. You talkin' a tricky fuckin' operation.

ACT ONE 23

RICKY: You can kill my ass, Augie, or maybe you can leave it to Mike. Or them niggers can kill my ass. It don't matter a shit to me, Augie, it don't.

(Pause)

CRANK: It don't matter a shit to Ricky, Augie.

(AUGIE *slowly turns from the window. Glares at* CRANK)

RICKY: Shut the fuck up, Crank.

AUGIE: *(To* CRANK*)* I tell Mike to kill the fat faggot first. I tell him to hang the fat fag by her big tits from the West Side Highway. *(Pause. To* RICKY*)* O K, big head. Let's say you pull it off with Mrs Roper. You still got this body stinkin' up my bed.

RICKY: Mike take care of that body. Who else?

AUGIE: How Mike take care of that body? Mike take care of that body he kill your ass.

RICKY: Maybe. Maybe not. It was some john cacked the kid. You ditn't know. I ditn't know. Roper he's not talkin'. It was some john outa the Haymarket. Mike get rid of dead whores before.

AUGIE: Roper tell Mike.

RICKY: Why he want Mike to know? He's enough trouble we know.

AUGIE: This a tricky fuckin' operation, greaseball. Roper gonna spring for a dead whore?

RICKY: Roper ain't gonna know. I say, the kid's so stoned he's out of it Mister Roper you can do whatever. Now Roper is out of it too, know what I mean? Dust.

AUGIE: Roper don't get dusted.

RICKY: Roper get dusted today. *(Pause)* So O K, maybe Roper ties the kid up—some weird shit. Maybe even tries to cut him a little—what the fuck? The kid is already dead, know what I mean? And Roper, Roper can't handle dust. I give him a few minutes. I come back, you know, I forget somethin'. Hey. I do this thing. Hey. What the fuck? The kid you know what I mean looks weird. Hey. Hey. Mister Roper. Hey. Jesus. Oh Jesus... The kid is dead. Roper can't handle dust.

(Pause)

AUGIE: You are some kinna somethin', greaseball.

RICKY: Then Roper gotta come across. Five fat G's.

AUGIE: How you know I don't call Mike, tell him there this greaser motherfuck got big plans middle of Mike's own fuckin' operation?

RICKY: Mike don't give you piddle shit, hey Augie? And you sick of it. Hey? *(Pause)* That why you gone last night? Saturday night is rip time. *(Pause)* Mike think I fuck him over he think *you* fuck him over. He maybe believe you you kill my ass. But you ain't killed nobody yet and you fuckin' ain't gonna kill me now. *(Pause)*

AUGIE: Half.

RICKY: One fuckin' third.

AUGIE: Half.

RICKY: One fuckin' third. Me. You. And Crank cause he do deliveries.

AUGIE: *(Nodding towards bed)* What about them two?

RICKY: *(Loudly)* Blow keeps his mouth shut he fuckin' peddles funerals. He end up dead too the street find out. Maybe we be nice to him let him carry a little.

(BLOW *does not respond.*)

RICKY: And Mitchell she hangs out with us. Hey. Mitchell. You hang out with us?

MITCHELL: I hang out with you since I'm sellin' my pussy.

ACT ONE   25

AUGIE: *(Peering out window)* Fuckin' jeez.

RICKY: *(To* AUGIE*)* I got no choice my ass is dead all kinds of people. Only I think maybe if it's my ass it's your ass too. And his. And hers. And his. *(Pause)*

AUGIE: Midnight.

RICKY: You can't wait the fuck till morning?

AUGIE: Midnight. *(Pause)* I come back at midnight. There's no coke there's no niggers. Just that stiff on the bed and my commission. I ain't been here all day. Settin' up a act. *(Turns from window; to* RICKY*)* You was in charge. I tell Mike, Ricky was in charge. Then *you* tell him that cocksuck story some john outa the Haymarket. *(Pause)* I ain't been this apartment.

RICKY: I handle Mike.

CRANK: But gotta cut it. Wrap it. Deliver it. By midnight, Ricky?

RICKY: Shut your fuck. *(Pause)*

AUGIE: Jeez. *(Pause)* Midnight. *(He crosses to door. Scans room)* I ain't been these facilities. *(He exits through entrance door.)*

CRANK: *(To* RICKY*)* That mother is got shit runnin' down his leg he so scared. Ricky? You scared him he got shit runnin' down his leg.

RICKY: *(Standing)* All I smell is sweat offa you—only you too stupid to be scared. We gotta move. You get your fat ass down to Forty-deuce. Tell them niggers to come later. Like at ten. They bitch? And you say fat five.

CRANK: What if they ain't in that armpit bar? What if they gone uptown?

RICKY: Then you go uptown.

CRANK: Ricky? I don't know from uptown. I never go above Ninety-sixth.

RICKY: Shit. Can you be this fuckin' stupid? Dyke hangs out that chili stand that pizza stand on Hunnert Twenny-fifth.

CRANK: Hunnert Twenny-fifth?

RICKY: On the corner. Right where you get off the subway all them niggers pukin' and shootin'. The I R T.

CRANK: The I R T you mean on the Square?

RICKY: Oh fuck. *(Pause)* Blow. It's that hop house that chili parlor pizza joint what the fuck on Hunnert Twenny-fifth?

(BLOW *continues staring at wall.*)

BLOW: There's a dead kid this apartment, Ricky.

RICKY: Blow. You answer the fuckin' question that dyke her old man.

(BLOW *does not respond.*)

RICKY: And after you answer the question then you get me some grass. Dust it kinna heavy, Blow, so Roper don't know the kid is cacked.

(BLOW *does not respond.*)

RICKY: Blow? *(Crosses to opposite side of bed)* Blow? *(Leans across bed. To* BLOW's *back)* Blow you mother.

BLOW: You hadda fuckin' kill him!

(RICKY *and* BLOW *stare at one another.*)

CRANK: You give us that slime. Hey. Ricky—

BLOW: *(To* CRANK*)* Up your ass, fat suck! *(Pause)* That kid ditn't do shit to shit. He come here this toilet cause his brother say he just a little queer get outa my house

my shitty wife and stupid kids. Some upstate crud, can you just see him?
RICKY: What you fuck?
(BLOW *arranges the sheet over* JOHN ANTHONY; *in so doing he pulls the sheet from under* RICKY'*s knee.*)
BLOW: Back off.
(RICKY *stands upright.*)
BLOW: Think he so straight prob'ly take it up the ass. I deal with straight guys they all take it up the ass. Then they go back to the wife and the girlfriend and talk about queers! They climb on toppa some cunt and sweat and shake. They can't come they say, Honey, put your finger up my ass please honey pop my ass. I pop your ass you bozo. I put my dick up your straight pussy so many times your old lady die laughin' she see you with your buns in the air! *(Pause)* I see him his buddies cruisin' B-way every goddamn night. Lookin' for cunt so weird—you know that come from nowhere look with the plaid shirts and the lettermen jackets they don't know it but they look like faggots. I cut one outa the pack—he so lame he say, Hey man know where I can get me some warm pussy? You know you gonna end up on toppa his butt grindin' in to him he squeak and moan like a doll you squeeze it! Then he go back to Utica throw out his little brother the little queer can't live with such a real fuckin' man and his real fuckin' wife and real fuckin' brats—just one big fuckin' T V show. Little brother too pretty too sexy for such a big bullshit stud. Fuck Ricky why you guys nail a spike in that kid's arm? *(Pause)* Ricky? Why you slip a needle in that tissue paper skin all them little blue veins how could you do that? Fuck Ricky how could you do that? *(He fiddles some more with the sheet. Discovers T-shirt among the folds)* Stupid tacky shirt. I get him this tacky motherfuck shirt. *(Pause)*

RICKY: You done yet? You finish with the funeral?

BLOW: You kill him and now you fuck, now you wanna sell him!

RICKY: *Who* kill the kid, Blow? *I* ditn't kill the kid. *You* kill the kid, Blow! So what you fuck I sell his dead ass?

(BLOW *sits on bed, staring at shirt.*)

RICKY: A buncha weird ones this apartment buncha dizzy queens don't you unnerstand? We gotta move. Or we gonna have broken glass rubbed in our eyes. Or maybe we get lucky only a coupla fingers bent back. By midnight we gotta have our shit all wrapped up and ready to deliver! Blow: dust. Crank: the niggers. Unnerstand?

CRANK: Yeah, Ricky.

BLOW: Shit.

RICKY: Unnerstand?

BLOW: Fuck O K. I unnerstand!

(Pause)

RICKY: O K. I'm gonna go into the bat'room. I will *not* be takin a shit. We gotta have a schedule you queens drivin' me crazy. Blow. One hour. Crank. I give you `til five. The rest of the schedule when I got it figured. You better both be here when I say. *(He crosses to bathroom door, enters, closes door.)*

MITCHELL: *(Looking at door)* Is that gonna be headquarters?

CRANK: Mitchell, how I get to Hunnert Twenny-fifth?

BLOW: It's Hunnert Ten. You come up the subway. Dyke's inna donut shop see her through the plate glass. *(He stands up. Carefully folds T-shirt and places it on bed)* Mitchell, you be here to watch the kid, right?

ACT ONE 29

MITCHELL: She goin' somewhere? Yeah I be here—where else?

BLOW: Keep the sheet over him he's naked?

MITCHELL: Such a father thing you got, Blow. Every twelve-year-old dump her ass on Forty-deuce Blow gotta listen to the big tragedy. Put his arm around her shoulders. Bring her T H C and franks from Nedick's—get what I mean—and then before you know it he's fuckin' her.

CRANK: Mitchell, how I get to Hunnert Twenny-fifth?

BLOW: One Ten, Crank.

MITCHELL: Go down to T-Square take the crosstown shuttle to Grand Central. Take the I R T uptown express to Eighty-sixth. Take the uptown local get off One Ten. *(Pause)*

CRANK: I come in from Brooklyn I R T.

MITCHELL: That's the *Seventh* Avenue I R T. You want the *Lex* I R T.

BLOW: Fuck, take the E or the A up Eighth Avenue.

MITCHELL: What the fuck he do that? He can't transfer uptown offa the I N D.

BLOW: So fuck it he go to Queens Plaza. There's two shuttles he prob'ly end up Queens anyhow.

CRANK: Oh fuck I don't wanna go to Queens, Mitchell.

MITCHELL: Take the crosstown, Crank, it stops at Grand Central. Blow's right. You take the Queensborough you end up Kew Gardens, Jamaica—some fuckin' place.

CRANK: Jesus I hope them niggers is down on Forty-deuce. How many fuckin' shuttles I have to ride?

MITCHELL: There's only one shuttle. Queensborough acts like a shuttle only she's not.

BLOW: Or hey. Take the N train or the Double R uptown at Forty-ninth. You get off at Fifty-ninth transfer to the Lex no problem.

MITCHELL: Look. The B M T goes out to Queens we got the same problem.

CRANK: Blow, I don't wanna go to Queens.

MITCHELL: Take the crosstown shuttle not the Queensborough and it fuckin' dies at Grand Central. End of the line. You can sit there all fuckin' day it will never go to Queens.

CRANK: I know how to take the B-way local. What happens I take that?

MITCHELL: You end up in the Bronx after about two weeks.

BLOW: Crank, come on. We go down to T-Square I got to connect. Prob'ly the dyke is in that bar?

MITCHELL: Well, you *could* take the B-way local uptown to Two Hunnert Fifteen. Then take the *downtown* to Hunnert and Ten and Lenox and walk over. Or hey—

(Bathroom door opens and RICKY *steps out.)*

RICKY: *Shit on the cocksuckin' subway, take a fuckin' bus! (Pause)* Up the rectum—I got dizzy queens up the rectum. Blow. Crank. Get your asses *on* the street! *On* the street!

BLOW: Don't push me Ricky—I ram your balls up your nose?

(Pause)

RICKY: You wanna handle this, bohunk? You handle this you end up two broken knees back on Tomkins Square. Old bohunk ladies grind out cigarettes in your face.

ACT ONE 31

BLOW: So? I go to Brooklyn your wop mother she suck my cock.

(Pause. They are nose to nose.)

RICKY: One halfa Tomkins Square is niggers. The other half is bohunks. The city oughta bomb it.

BLOW: All them greasy wops in Brooklyn how come it don't slide inna ocean?

RICKY: You got a hour, Blow.

BLOW: You make me laugh, Ricky. This all crazy—the niggers and the kid. Get ahold of Roper. Cram the deal. Go downtown.

RICKY: All my life somebody tryin' to keep me from getting mine.

MITCHELL: Jesus Ricky so what are you? Seventeen?

RICKY: *ALL MY FUCKIN' LIFE!*

(There is a long silence, as BLOW *and* RICKY *stare at each other.)*

CRANK: *(To* MITCHELL*)* Anyhow I don't fuckin' hafta go uptown?

MITCHELL: *(Looking at* RICKY*)* You'd of gone the fuck to Queens.

CRANK: *(To* MITCHELL*)* I never was in Queens. This john once he wanted me to go out there his place. In his car? Said he woulda take me this Chinese restaurant. Can you feature me some Chinese restaurant in Queens? With this old john and the forksticks and eggrolls and shit? *(Pause)* Ricky? Out to fuckin' Queens?

*(*RICKY *turns abruptly from* BLOW *and stalks into bathroom, slamming the door behind him.)*

*(*BLOW *crosses slowly to bed, staring at the body. He turns and sinks onto the bed's margin.)*

(Silence)

(Lights out)

END OF ACT ONE

ACT TWO

Scene One

(Night)

(JOHN ANTHONY's twisted form, beneath the sheet, is vivid on the bed in the darkened room.)

(RICKY is sitting in a chair stage right of the bed, staring at the body.)

RICKY: *(To the body)* I know I first see you you was gonna bust my balls. You gonna take me with you? Hey. You fetus?

(There is a knocking at the door.)

RICKY: Night before last you was upstate prob'ly some treehouse playin' all the other kids. Lakes and rivers and woods and shit, all that like the Catskills. I was the Catskills once.

(There is a louder knocking.)

RICKY: It's funny, New York. Some kids cute like you they come Manhattan make three, four bills a week. Happens. But you come here you fuckin' cack first time you suck a needle.

(There is a rattling of the door.)

RICKY: Now I'm tellin' you you gotta come through for me. You come here to get your own and you fuck up. So now you get me mine.

(*Pounding at door.* BLOW's *voice.* "Ricky!" RICKY *rises, goes to door. Admits* BLOW. RICKY *returns to chair by bed, glumly staring at body as before.* BLOW *closes door, hesitates, then moves to bed, on the margin of which he sits, facing* RICKY. BLOW *throws a lid of grass on* RICKY's *lap.*)

BLOW: She smoke enough a that you can show movies between her tits.

(RICKY *does not respond; he continues to stare at the body throughout most of the remaining dialogue.*)

BLOW: Hey. I brung it like you ask?

RICKY: So O K. So now what you fuck? Go down the Haymarket hang out Crank and Mitchell. They come back when the niggers get here.

BLOW: I hang out right here.

RICKY: You fuck you hang out here.

BLOW: You gonna handle Roper?

RICKY: I handle everything. I don't want you here Roper come, Blow.

BLOW: It don't take long Roper know the kid is cacked.

RICKY: He stoned so bad who knows? I figure five, ten minutes he get into somethin'—it don't matter what.

BLOW: You better make it five minutes, Ricky.

RICKY: Just to be alone this room with the fetus, that's all it takes.

BLOW: Maybe even two minutes, Ricky.

RICKY: He don't have to think he kill the kid's ass you know with his own fuckin' hands. Just you know to *be* here. Then I come back he got to buy his way out. This one will handle Roper, Blow.

BLOW: So how much you tell him to bring? You promise the niggers five G's.

ACT TWO

RICKY: You don't tell a guy like Roper how much. You just say I got this specialty piece of very young chicken anyway got to bring a wad of C notes. That's all the nigger needs to see. It don't matter Roper got the card.

(Pause)

BLOW: The card?

RICKY: The card you know you go to this bank day or night shove it in money comes out. You know them automatic machines, bills come shootin' out.

BLOW: What, you march him down to some machine?

RICKY: Everything is by machine. You put your card inna slot. The bank door opens. We go in. He put the card this one machine it tell him how much he got. I want five G's to start the job. He go to this other machine he tell it how much we need. Hey. Machine. Get your fuckin' ass in gear I want five round ones. Machine go, sure, why the fuck not? All these bills pop out.

BLOW: What you, march him down to some machine he dusted to the tits?

(Pause)

RICKY: So anyway he got to bring a buncha C's that keep the nigger happy til I use the fuckin' card. I don't want you here Roper come, Blow.

BLOW: You just gonna have him see the kid like this?

RICKY: So?

(BLOW *stands by bed and very tenderly arranges the boy's body beneath the sheet so that it appears to be sleeping, the head partially exposed and nestled into a pillow.*)

BLOW: He shouldn't *look* like a dead body.

RICKY: Some off the roof got some weird for this dead fuckin' fetus.

BLOW: *(Sitting on bed again.)* I help you get Roper dusted he get here. You need me, Ricky.

RICKY: My asshole.

BLOW: You need me for Roper. I *do* Roper. I *know* Roper.

RICKY: *(Looking at BLOW for the first time.)* What you want from me, Blow?

BLOW: You let me set him up, Ricky, so he don't find out the kid is dead.

RICKY: You gonna mess me, Blow, this crazy shit with the fetus?

BLOW: Crazy so what?

RICKY: I handle it, Blow.

BLOW: She laugh at you, Ricky. Your deal go down the toilet.

RICKY: I was a player, Blow, East New York. This girl was so hot for me—

BLOW: Shit, Ricky.

(Pause)

RICKY: So O K. O K, *bohunk*. I'm gonna let you stay. I'm gonna let you stay know why?

BLOW: Why, Ricky?

RICKY: So you can face it, Blow. So you can face I am runnin' this deal.

(Pause)

BLOW: Sure, Ricky.

(RICKY *throws lid at* BLOW.)

RICKY: Now roll a couple.

BLOW: Yeah, O K, Ricky. *(He begins rolling joints.)*

RICKY: So lissen to me, Blow. We got to hot Roper up.

ACT TWO

BLOW: Who the fuck you talkin' to, Ricky?

RICKY: We got to get him so hot he don't look at the kid so close 'til we leave. So hot maybe he give head to one of us.

BLOW: Ditn't I tell you Roper bounce off the wall, Ricky?

RICKY: He won't be so cocksuckin' smooth he get fucked up.

BLOW: You handle this dust, Ricky?

RICKY: I got a choice?

BLOW: This stuff black and white you know what I mean? It hits you like speed. Everything goes black, except for the lights, and they like go white.

RICKY: Shitface.

BLOW: Roper gets most of it anyway. You toke, he toke. I toke, he toke. You toke, he toke. Know what I mean?

(There is a knocking at the door, three evenly spaced thumps.)

RICKY: *(Standing)* The john.

(RICKY goes to door. Admits ROPER, who is carrying a briefcase. RICKY leads ROPER back to the bed.)

RICKY: Hey. Mister Roper. Have a seat.

(ROPER remains standing, peering around the room. Sets down briefcase.)

ROPER: Why is it so dark in here?

RICKY: We was getting' stoned. You member Blow?

BLOW: Hey, Mister Roper.

ROPER: Of course. How are you, Blow? We had a session, when was it? Several months ago. Why is it so dark in here?

RICKY: We was getting' stoned, the kid got wrecked. Fuckin' out of it. Have a seat, Mister Roper?

(ROPER *remains standing. He eyes* JOHN ANTHONY's *body.)*

ROPER: How wrecked is "wrecked"?

RICKY: Fuck you know he's just in from upstate. What a twelve-year-old kid know from good dope in fuckin' Utica?

ROPER: Looks like a nice kid.

BLOW: A sweetheart, Mister Roper.

ROPER: Have you fucked him, Blow?

RICKY: Hey. Mister Roper. I tell you the kid is fresh. Nobody lay his dirty fingers—

ROPER: Yes, of course, Ricky. *(He seats himself next to bed, in chair previously occupied by* RICKY.*)* So tell me, Blow, how is it going? I've often wondered what became of you.

BLOW: I'm O K, Mister Roper. But I'm gonna be better after this joint. It's the horniest fuckin' grass I ever smoke.

ROPER: Really? The boy doesn't seem at all excited.

RICKY: He been smokin all day waitin' for you. I hadda give him somethin' to do so I feed him this shit like it was pretzels?

ROPER: How horny, Blow, did the kid get?

BLOW: I don't know I'm in and out.

RICKY: Hot as a firecracker, Mister Roper. Lay there strokin' himself. Now he's like fuckin' putty.

ROPER: Yeah? Well, I'd like to take a look in a moment, if it's all right with you, Blow.

RICKY: What the fuck with Blow?

ACT TWO   39

ROPER: Well, I assume it's Blow who broke him in. It usually is you, isn't it, Blow?

RICKY: Ditn't I tell you? The kid's fresh.

BLOW: Ricky's right, Mister Roper. *(He lights a joint.)* Have a toke, Mister Roper?

(ROPER accepts the joint.)

ROPER: Why not, if it's as good as you say?

RICKY: Mister Roper. I would lie to you? You a businessman. This one a businessman. Satisfaction guaranteed.

ROPER: *(Toking between sentences.)* A businessman, Ricky, is one who has a product to sell or a product to buy. A consultant, who is not a businessman, places the two in relation. I am a consultant. I dislike, I even a little resent, being made to barter like a Puerto Rican shill. For some discount shop. On Fourteenth Street. *You* understand me, don't you, Blow?

RICKY: What the fuck with Blow?

ROPER: I can't imagine *what*, the other week, you were doing in front of Exxon, Blow. You couldn't have been more conspicuously out of place. *(He remembers the joint in his fingers.)* Oh. *(Hands joint to RICKY. To BLOW)* Did you suppose I'd think you cute for leering at me?

(RICKY tokes quickly and hands joint back to ROPER.)

RICKY: Blow is very uncool sometimes, Mister Roper. Me, I am always cool.

BLOW: Hey. Mister Roper. You was alone, wadn't you?

ROPER: *(Toking)* I am never alone on Sixth Avenue, Blow. *(He hands joint to BLOW who tokes and hands it back.)*

RICKY: Hey. Mister Roper. You don't have to worry, this kid is top quality product.

ROPER: Top quality product. Indeed. *(Toking)* Augie should be in on this conversation. He likes talking "product." I indulge him of course. Do you know why, Blow?

BLOW: No, Mister Roper. Why?

ROPER: Well, sometimes I think that treating you kids as "product" is our way of keeping you at arm's length. On Sixth Avenue, it's one thing, don't you see? One is indifferent to particulars. But on Eighth Avenue we cannot really, I mean not really, be free from particular sorts of sensations involving particular sorts of boys. Hence the vocabulary of commodities. A distancing device. *(He remembers the joint in his fingers.)* Oh. *(He tokes and hands joint to* RICKY. *He is mechanically echoing the same action he performed earlier.)* I keep forgetting you're there, Ricky.

*(*RICKY *tokes hastily and at once hands joint back to* ROPER.*)*

RICKY: That's O K, Mister Roper.

ROPER: You're not terribly appreciative of this dope, are you, Ricky?

RICKY: Just like the kid I smoke it all day. *(Gestures towards* JOHN ANTHONY*)* Take a look. Blow, get up so's he can take a look.

ROPER: In a moment, Blow. *(He tokes and passes joint to* BLOW.*)* The word is "product", kids. We can't after all admit to being in your power. It was the feeling of being without power that made me hurt you, Blow.

BLOW: *(Toking; coldly)* You ditn't hurt me, Mister Roper.

ROPER: Didn't I? You seemed so—well, so upset at the time.

*(*BLOW *passes joint to* ROPER.*)*

BLOW: Part of the fuckin' scene, man.

ACT TWO   41

ROPER: What? Oh, I think I see. You acted upset because I *wanted* you to act upset. *(Toking)* Or rather, you *thought* I *wanted* you to act upset.

BLOW: Hey, Mister Roper. You get off?

ROPER: By which you mean, don't you, that so long as I derive pleasure from your reaction it doesn't matter what I want your reaction to be? In short, you modulate my desires?

BLOW: Hey. Mister Roper. What you want from me?

ROPER: You see, Blow, that's exactly what I'm talking about. I derive the most intense pleasure from knowing that your body is being purchased in the same way as toothpaste or a pair of shoes. It's tit for tat, kids. Our tyranny as opposed to yours. *(He remembers the joint in his fingers.)* Oh. *(Mechanically again, a bit too mechanically, he tokes and passes joint to* RICKY, *whom he does not look at.)* Your fucking stomach, Blow.

BLOW: Hey. What's the point, Mister Roper?

*(*RICKY *tokes quickly and holds joint towards* ROPER, *who does not notice.)*

ROPER: Your slightly swollen belly. It was hard, it was muscular, but it was also a trifle bloated. In a very sexy way.

(Pause)

BLOW: Hey, forget it, Mister Roper.

ROPER: It was asking to be ravaged. White and firm as a mound of butter. And then the streak of blood. *(Pause)*

RICKY: *(Looking at* BLOW*)* Jesus. *(He forgetfully raises joint to his lips, tokes, remembers, and nervously extends it towards* ROPER *again.)* Mister Roper.

ROPER: *(Taking joint)* I couldn't show up at the office for a week. *(Toking)* Blow, always direct your fists at a man's body, where the damage won't be noticeable.

(ROPER *passes joint to* BLOW.)

BLOW: I ditn't hurt your fucking face, Mister Roper. That was all in your head. I just slap you around a little. *(With a pronounced shrug)* Know what I mean?

(BLOW *has not toked; passes joint to* ROPER.)

ROPER: No, I *don't* know what you mean, Blow. *(He begins aping* BLOW's *shrug, markedly overdoing it.)* How *could* I know? Did you know I spent a week with a certain doctor out on the Island? *(He is shrugging wildly now.)* No, kiddo, I *don't* know what you mean. What *do* you mean, Blow? Are you calling me a liar, Blow? What do you mean, Blow?

RICKY: Whyn't you tell Augie, Mister Roper? Or Mike? They break his fuckin' arm.

(ROPER *is suddenly quiet.*)

ROPER: This J has gone out.

RICKY: Wait 'til you see this one, Mister Roper. You think Blow got a stomach—

ROPER: *(To* RICKY*)* I told you this J has gone out.

RICKY: Hey. Blow. A match for Mister Roper.

(BLOW *takes joint from* ROPER*, lights it, and hands it back.*)

BLOW: Come on, Mister Roper. This shit I don't feature. You wanna play with razor blades you shoulda let me know before, that's all. But even so what I do? I don't break your face. I break your face like Ricky says you get me killed.

ROPER: *(Toking)* Next time I *will* have you killed.

BLOW: *(Laughing)* Hey, Mister Roper. *(Cups his crotch with hand)* What you want—you wanna suck my cock?

RICKY: Yeah, Mister Roper, don't be shy. Suck his fuckin' cock. We'll have a party.

ROPER: A party, Ricky? No one's going to touch *you*.

ACT TWO 43

(Pause)

RICKY: Hey. Blow. Show Mister Roper the merchandise.

ROPER: *(Toking)* The "merchandise". You're not Jewish, are you, Ricky?

BLOW: Mister Roper, you don't grow up New York?

ROPER: Why do you ask, Blow?

BLOW: Shit, Ricky and me we grow up New York.

ROPER: *(Toking)* And therefore—?

BLOW: *(Shrugging)* You know.

(ROPER *begins shrugging grotesquely again.*)

ROPER: *What* do I know? Tell me. What?

RICKY: The kid's from upstate, Mister Roper.

BLOW: Mister Roper, you from upstate?

ROPER: Why do you ask, Blow?

BLOW: I don't know, Mister Roper.

ROPER: Why do you ask, Blow? *(Pause. He is shrugging crazily.)* Why do you ask? Why do you ask, Blow?

BLOW: Well, you know, me and Ricky ain't the same as you.

(ROPER *is suddenly quiet. Tokes and passes joint to* BLOW)

ROPER: I don't understand what you're trying to say. Are you trying to say that growing up in New York makes a person obnoxious? Makes him small and ugly and cheap?

RICKY: Hey. Mister Roper. So what's it like upstate? Like the Catskills, right? My people drive to the Catskills one summer I was a kid.

ROPER: Oh, *that* must have been fun. A trail of beer cans. Pizza rinds. Prosciutto. Wax paper. Olive pits. All the way to Woodstock.

(Pause. BLOW, *who hasn't toked, hands joint to* ROPER.*)*

RICKY: You grow up Utica, Mister Roper? The kid's from Utica.

ROPER: I grew up, Ricky, in Connecticut.

BLOW: Hey, Mister Roper. I think you must be horny. You wanna bite cock, Mister Roper? Then somebody rip you back, make you come.

ROPER: I am not horny, Blow, in the least. *(Tokes, looks at joint, and places it in ashtray on the floor.)* This grass is lethal.

(BLOW *places another joint in his mouth.)*

BLOW: Hey. Let's do another one. Get fucked up.

ROPER: I never abdicate control, Blow, when I'm messing with trade. Part of the attraction is that you're unpredictable.

(BLOW *begins pawing himself.)*

BLOW: Hey. Mister Roper. I can see you now. Down on your fuckin' knees lickin' my thighs. I say, Hey, Mister Roper, you gettin me wet. You don't slobby my balls my cock. You clean my asshole, maybe. *(Spreading legs)* That's right, Roper, up my shitty asshole—you can't have my cock you pussy. *(To* RICKY*)* Then Roper get mad, you know what I mean?

RICKY: Sure. Roper's no kinna guy licks dirty asshole.

BLOW: *(Lighting joint)* Fuck no. So he start to pinch and slap and grab. He jab his thumb up my asshole I start to yell.

RICKY: His fuckin' fingernail rippin' your asshole.

ACT TWO   45

BLOW: Rippin' my asshole *inside* my asshole. Cuttin' me inside, man. That's what hots up Mister Roper. Hey. Mister Roper. *(Deadly)* That's what hots you up. Inside.

(BLOW *passes joint to* ROPER, *who accepts it but does not toke.*)

ROPER: You guys should go on television.

RICKY: The whole thing is inside, that's the whole thing about it.

(ROPER, *without toking, extends joint towards* RICKY.)

RICKY: *(Quickly)* Hey. No. No thanks, man.

(ROPER *extends joint towards* BLOW.)

ROPER: Blow?

BLOW: You take it, Mister Roper. Right, that's the whole thing. You can whip some motherfuck or you can cut him or you can chaindance on his face. But it's inside, that's where you got to go.

RICKY: That's what we sell, man. We don't sell our outsides what you fuck?

BLOW: Right. Don't sell ass or cock. Sell tickets to our insides. The liver, all them rubbery round things, your fuckin' spine and shit.

ROPER: *(Toking)* Television. That's exactly the medium.

BLOW: Come on, Ricky.

RICKY: Hey. Mister Roper. You can go through every catalog this town you won't find pussy this sweet this young this hot.

ROPER: I'm sure I won't, Ricky.

RICKY: Know what the kid tell me today? He say he gonna get so out of it that what he wants he wants to wake up and see some guy doin' him. And then you know he can't stop it, just lay there through the whole thing. Nothin' you can't do to him he fuckin' *wants* you to do shit to him. If he was just a hooker Mister Roper he give out with limits. But this kid Mister Roper he wants *you* to find his limits.

BLOW: What's this shit, Ricky? Mister Roper knows what he wants.

ROPER: *(Toking)* His body is too white.

RICKY: So what you want—a nigger?

ROPER: This grass is... *(He throws joint in the ashtray.)*

RICKY: Hey. Mister Roper. *(He crosses to other side of bed, to stand by chair looking at* ROPER.*)* Look. I charge you what you think is fair. You do him a little. You don't like it you come downstairs I'm at the Haymarket.

ROPER: The body is too white. The sheets are too white. The whole thing is sickening.

(Pause while RICKY *and* BLOW *exchange looks.)*

BLOW: Look, Mister Roper. You think now you think it make you throw up. It always comes off like that at first.

RICKY: Sure. But you get into it later.

BLOW: I know you, Mister Roper. You ain't like them other johns. Rubbin' up against me and actin' like a bitch. But you actin like a bitch now, Mister Roper, and that ain't you—you fuckin' get tired with that. You a man, Mister Roper. A man has got to be master. That's why you like guys. Every cocksuck can make a bitch do his shit. But here's this kid. And he sayin' to you, O K man show me some cock. I been dreamin' about this, now you take me down the street you show me some cock.

RICKY: Sure. These little out-of-town numbers the hardest ones. They been savin' it up inside like if you

ACT TWO

ditn't jack off for twelve years that's what this kid is like. You be sorry you don't try it, Mister Roper.

BLOW: You be sorry later, Mister Roper. You a man, Mister Roper, and you got to show this kid some real fuckin' cock.

RICKY: He never see real fuckin' cock, Mister Roper, not like you gonna show him.

BLOW: No shit cock, Mister Roper.

RICKY: Real motherfuckin' cock, Mister Roper.

ROPER: *(Screaming)* GET OUT! *(Pause. Covers his face with his hands)*

RICKY: Sure, Mister Roper.

BLOW: O K, Mister Roper.

*(*RICKY *and* BLOW *move towards door, pause, look back at* ROPER. BLOW *looks anxiously at bed. The boys exit. After a pause* ROPER *drops his hands and looks about him in the darkness, hugging himself.)*

ROPER: Why is it so dark in here? *(Suddenly, he stands; looks down at* JOHN ANTHONY.*)* That's right. Just lie there. *(Pause. Then he begins to pace to and fro before the bed as he speaks.)* Never overdo the drugs when you're dealing with trade. On the other hand, I feel so stupid if I don't take my share. *(Mumbling)* Why do I sound so pathetic? *(To* JOHN ANTHONY*)* You see yourself how strong this grass is. Dynamite, isn't that the word? Nitroglycerine. I tell myself, you ass, don't keep toking away like a chimney. At first you feel so powerful. Then so afraid. *(Mumbling)* Only one joint, I'm falling to pieces over one joint? *(He halts abruptly.)* Was it treated with something? Blow wouldn't dare. I'd have him killed. *(Resumes pacing. To* JOHN ANTHONY*)* Killed, do you understand? I've been a customer on these streets for years. This is New York City, kiddo. You put out, you produce, you deliver. *(Suddenly giggling)* Such

a by god movie. Everything you feel, every thought
you express, it's like a pound of pastrami laid on a deli
counter. *(Goofing)* Is it fresh? Of course it's fresh.
Would we sell you meat wasn't one hunnert percent
fresh? Listen, we make a *nice* sandwich. *(Mumbling)*
That wasn't coherent. *(To* JOHN ANTHONY*)* Why do I
say things like, "Part of your attraction, my dear Blow,
is that you are unpredictable"? Did you hear that? No
wonder I get laughed at behind my back by these
twats. Behind my back? Blow was laughing at me right
to my *face*. *(Halts)* He's a good lay, that boy. Isn't he?
Well, it's going to be a bit rougher with me, kiddo.
(Resumes pacing) Now, poppers, I like poppers. Or
coke. Coke and poppers, they're all body. But grass,
I've never gotten used to it, sometimes it's so totally a
matter of the thoughts, the fears, the little needling
doubts. Like acid, like...like all those *mind*-fucking
drugs. Of course, you just let your fears, I suppose the
word is, vomit out of you. Normally I don't carry on
like this, this grass is very, as you know very... That's
right. Just lie there. *(Pause as he stares down at* JOHN
ANTHONY*)* I brought some toys, kiddo. I may just
handcuff you to the bed. *(He goes to briefcase, opens it,
pauses.)* Only I don't believe I'm going to fuck you after
all. Too bad. *(Pauses. Resumes pacing)* You're lying there
expecting me to tear into you, aren't you? You think by
playing dead animal I'll really make a mess of you,
don't you? Well, think again, kiddo. You don't excite
me at all. You disgust me. *(Halts; looks about him)* God,
it's dark in here. *(Resumes pacing)* Actually I rather
enjoy these sleazy pits. Not for the cliché reasons, I
assure you. Not because I have a hard-on for filth, not
because I'm slumming, like some oleomargarine
leather queen. *(Mumbling)* Am I even in the slightest
degree coherent? *(Abruptly laughing)* I like the drama of
it, goddamn it. I *like* sitting here with these cheap little
tarts and putting on a show! I *like* playing roles. Oh,

ACT TWO   49

you'll learn about playing parts if you stick around
New York City, kiddo! Sometimes, with a client, I'll
give him a taste of something besides the "exquisite
bland". I did *not* come off the parking lot and rise to be
president of the corporation. *Not* some glossy puppet,
acquiring all those funny mannerisms such a creature
thinks is required. I'm an independent, essentially. I
have the correct background, and I'm told it shows. I
am *not* smooth. Effortless. There's a subtle difference.
Impeccably businesslike, don't you know, but
effortless. My mind is really—it literally glares at
them!—engaged with them only at the most superficial
level. *(Halts. Resumes pacing)* No, the structure of, what
shall I call it? Painful intimacy. Intimacy always is
painful. It has taken me years to discover that. Getting
painfully close to someone in this town is a bit
unsubtle? Yes, decidedly unsubtle for my taste. *(Halts.
Hugs himself.)* Cold in here. Middle of August and I'm
cold. Those sheets, I'm sure those sheets haven't been
washed in months. Yet they're blinding me. Like your
body. The sun comes out, suddenly everything aches,
everything is colder. Very disagreeable. *(Pause)*
Snow...I'm talking about snow. *(Resumes pacing.
Mumbling)* Something's wrong. *(To* JOHN ANTHONY*)* I
don't usually carry on like this. Some grass, hey kiddo?
(Pause) That's right. Just lie there. Nothing, kiddo, is
more boring than pointless motion! *(Resumes pacing)* I
would describe Blow as plump, wouldn't you? Rosy,
plump and frozen solid. Rather like a perfect small
fowl you might pick up at the supermarket. Naturally I
don't mean to make you jealous. There is a clientele for
your sort, believe me. And this silent fuck-me routine
is even more seductive. What's this? *(Discovers T-shirt
among sheets)* Is this part of your drag, honey? The Big
Apple? It's actually a big banana, Mary, and they'll
ram it right up your uterus. *(Mumbling)* Who said that?
Who in hell delivered *that* line? *(To* JOHN ANTHONY.*)*

Put it on. *(Throws T-shirt at body.)* Put it on. I want you naked from the waist down. *(Pause)* Put it on. *(Pause)* I told you to put it on. *(Pause)* Put it on! *(Clutches T-shirt, slaps body with it.)* Put it on put it on put it on! Know what I mean? *(He begins wildly shrugging again.)* Know what I mean? Do you? Hey, man, youse know what I fuckin' mean? *(Throws T-shirt at body. Abruptly begins pacing again.)* Passion in grown men—don't you think?—is never quite real. Passion, the real stinking hots, spring from the child in us. You kids are very close to that. But there must be something fierce and dominant, too. Something I can provoke, and then break. That's where you lose, kiddo. Now, Blow...now Blow understands. *(Halts.)* Blow might have done very well, if he'd had half a chance. Had the right clothes, the right background, the right tone. *(Abruptly, he sits in chair by bed. Shakily lights a cigarette)* The world I move in, well, it's a tad abstract. Everything changes hands—money, whole corporations, people's careers and yet there's only the sound of paper rasping against fingertips. Only the vaguest of connections, you know. But you kids...you're such wonderfully foul little creatures. So very *alive*. In my world, kiddo, I sometimes think the fellows themselves were spawned in the bowels of Xerox machines. Still there is a kind of grace, an unconscious flowing ease, among those who gain control over others. To see it, kiddo, is as important as having it. When I encounter it—as I did the other day, a lawyer, in admiralty, patents, bankruptcy, anyhow some really shabby corner of the legal profession. This fellow had it all. Moved like a dream. Yet an abrupt boyishness. His grin was positively sardonic. *(Pause)* Does he go home on the 6:15 and dandle little waxen creatures on his knee? The wife, oh yes, there's a wife in there somewhere. Petite, blonde, skinny, wonderfully blank expression. Her voice crackles like potato chips. Kelly green lawns, the

ACT TWO

fine spray of sprinklers, a tricycle overturned, a Chris Craft in the driveway. I'm not, kiddo, putting it down. *Not* one of your sour city queens. There must be these differences, these several motivations. He plays the game for the good of his little family; it's a hallowed tradition, and I don't dispute it. It's simply that there are, don't you know, higher motivations. Finer vibrations. For the family man, you see, it's the money he's after, the security. He doesn't see the process for the forest of bucks. And the process, kiddo, is the most beautiful thing in the world. *(He stands up abruptly and begins pacing again.)* It can take greed, lust, fraud, every conceivable vileness, and produce not only the wealth, not only the action and purpose and point, but all the amenity, all the grace, all the complication that makes for interest, that makes for life. You learn to refine as it refines. You learn to see past the throngs of little hustlers with their warts and styes and meanness, their tiny bunkered deals. They're simply the what-do-you-call-'em? The ratchets and sprockets of an immense process that knows what it wants, that dices and selects and arranges according to its own lights. People keep looking for gods to worship. But they're already living in God's belly! When once you see it, it's exhilarating. Through all this there is this grace. Now that lawyer— *he* was capable of seeing it. But he fell for babies made of styrofoam and pineapple sundae wives. He fell short of the vision. *(Halts)* That's what one wants, kiddo. Someone at one's own level. Someone who understands. *(He sits in chair again.)* There *is* this grace. *(He leans forward, hugging himself.)* I swear there's an icicle down my spine. *(Rises and begins pacing again)* You saw of course what Blow was doing? That cheap device of digging at one's masculinity—in his hands it really amounts to a kind of satanism. The little twat. *(Begins twitching)* I took away *his* phony manhood the last time. Just reached up and—slit!—he had his first period! He brings it out of me. He's some kind of devil, some kind of filthy little devil. Popped his cherry, though, popped it good. God, the color of blood on that swelling skin. For a moment he just looked at me, big startled eyes. He was a little boy all of a sudden, it was as if I'd maimed a child. I wanted.... *(Halts, shivering)* I wanted to take him in my arms. I wanted to comfort him. *(Pacing again)* That's how we have it. Blow understands that. The kid screams. You gather him in your arms. That's how we have it. Like I say— he'd have made fine management. *(Pause)* But Blow is a twat. Oh, he knows how we have it. It's not that he hasn't played the battered boy for a thousand clients. But he wants to direct the show. The clients don't know it, maybe, but *he* has to be in charge. *(To* JOHN ANTHONY.*)* Well, nobody's in charge of *me*, kiddo. *(Halts. Shivers violently. Stares at* JOHN ANTHONY*)* I'm so cold... Please... Don't think badly of me... *(He climbs into bed; huddles under sheet, nestling against* JOHN ANTHONY's *body.)* That's right. Just lie there.

(Silence)

(Lights down)

Scene Two

(The same, a few moments later. Lights rise once again to glow on the bed, on the entwined forms beneath the sheet. There is the rasp of the automatic lock, and RICKY *and* BLOW *enter tentatively through entrance door.)*

RICKY: Hey. Mister Roper? *(Pause)* I forgot somethin', Mister Roper. In the bat'room? *(He approaches bed.)* Will you fuckin' look at this?

BLOW: I don't have to look.

RICKY: Hey. Mister Roper. *(He shakes* ROPER's *body.)* He's out of it.

ACT TWO

BLOW: You smoke that shit like he did you be out of it too.

(RICKY *lifts the sheet, then drops it.*)

RICKY: Like a coupla babies.

(BLOW *moves downstage to inspect the opened briefcase.*)

BLOW: He hardly even touch the toys. All this shit packed in here like his mother was sendin' him to summer camp.

RICKY: I figure he have the kid hangin' by his balls.

BLOW: Roper? —Shit.

RICKY: How you know that?

BLOW: I know Roper.

RICKY: Blow, he fuckin' cut you.

BLOW: Shit. You know what it was like? She was lickin' my balls and then it was like she goes— *(Gestures limply)* "Take that, Mary." Like with this blade she had hid in her fist. She just scratch me so I would beat the fuck outa her.

RICKY: You crazy, Blow.

(RICKY *stares at* BLOW, *then abruptly begins shaking* ROPER.)

RICKY: Hey. Roper. Jesus. Mister Roper. Hey. The kid, Mister Roper. What the fuck did you do? *(Pause)* Hey. Fuck. The kid is dead!

BLOW: She's gone uptown, Ricky. She gonna be there awhile. I got the shakes I don't even smoke half.

RICKY: I don't smoke it anyhow I'm fucked up from last night.

BLOW: You leave my dope in the bat'room?

RICKY: My fit. Your dope. How long before she come around? *(He sits in chair by the bed.)* I give her a few minutes. You get weird maybe but you don't get wrecked like this.

BLOW: That was strong shit, Ricky.

(*Again* RICKY *stares at* BLOW. *Then he leans forward, addressing* ROPER.)

RICKY: The kid is dead, Mister Roper. What we gonna do? Hey, Mister Roper. What the fuck we gonna do?

BLOW: Would you fuck off with that shit?

RICKY: (*To* BLOW) You do deliveries for me? Upper East? I can't send Crank Upper East.

BLOW: You don't got it yet, Ricky.

RICKY: It's in the pocket. (*He rises, bends over bed and rummages under the sheet; withdraws* ROPER's *wallet. Looks through it*) What's *this* bullshit. There's what there's maybe what? A halfa fuckin' C in her purse! What she think I gonna *bill* her?

BLOW: Mike prob'ly does.

(RICKY *begins violently shaking and slapping* ROPER.)

RICKY: Hey. You bitch. Get the fuck up! The kid is dead you bitch! I gotta get her outa here, now you get up!

(ROPER *stiffens under the blows, eyes open wildly.*)

ROPER: Please.

RICKY: You fuckin' asshole you get me in a shitty mess! You get me in a shitty mess you fuckin' asshole!

ROPER: Please.

RICKY: This ain't gonna be cheap, you cocksuck you pussy!

ROPER: (*Screaming*) Please! (*He curls into a tight ball and buries his head in the pillows.*)

(RICKY *drops into chair.*)

ACT TWO

RICKY: I give her a few minutes. We take the card, we go downstairs.

BLOW: How you gonna get her down to talk to some machine? She screamin' and shakin, and you say— Hey. Machine. My friend she's out of it but anyway you bitch put out. Hey. You bitch. Put the fuck out. Who crazy, Ricky? *You* crazy, Ricky.

RICKY: Shut your fuck, Blow.

(Pause)

BLOW: Niggers be here wantin' fat five, and you ain't even got one.

RICKY: Shut your fuck, Blow. *(Pause)* Why you get it so strong? *(Pause)* Blow? What else you got in there?

BLOW: Dust, man. Dust.

RICKY: Dust don't turn you no babyshit.

BLOW: Some people disco on this shit.

RICKY: What else you got in there, bohunk!

(When BLOW does not respond, RICKY abruptly rises and attacks ROPER again.)

RICKY: You pussy I gotta have five Gs I gotta have five Gs you pussy!

(He tries to pull ROPER from bed.)

(ROPER, his eyes shut, rolls over and grasps JOHN ANTHONY's body.)

RICKY: Get your pussy up you fuck!

BLOW: Stop that shit, Ricky.

RICKY: *(Still pulling at ROPER)* Five Gs five Gs five Gs.

(BLOW crosses to bed and shoves RICKY aside, then begins struggling with ROPER.)

BLOW: Get your fuckin' hands *offa* him, Roper!

(BLOW *disengages* ROPER *from* JOHN ANTHONY.)

ROPER: *(Screaming)* Please!

BLOW: You don't touch that kid you hear me, Roper?

(BLOW *pulls* ROPER *from the bed onto the floor.*)

(ROPER *in panic scrambles under bed.*)

RICKY: *(To* BLOW*)* So what you fuck? Now how I get him outa there?

BLOW: He don't touch the kid, that's all.

RICKY: The kid is dead, asshole!

BLOW: He don't touch him, that's all.

(RICKY *drops on his knees to shout under bed.*)

RICKY: Get outa there you pussy! Oh Jesus.

BLOW: That nigger cut you good, Ricky, you don't got somethin to show him.

(RICKY *manages to drag* ROPER *from beneath bed.* ROPER *is wound in a tight ball, fists crossed over chest, chin pressed into arms, eyes closed.*)

RICKY: *(Placating.)* Roper. Listen. I gotta go down to the bank. What's the code number for this fuckin' card?

(ROPER *does not respond.*)

RICKY: The code number. Mister Roper. Hey. The number.

(ROPER *wriggles back under the bed.*)

RICKY: Oh Jesus.

BLOW: Code number?

RICKY: Gotta have the code you punch in the number.

BLOW: What the fuck, you need a number? She can't tell you her address, and you got to have a number?

(RICKY *stands; abruptly sits in chair.*)

ACT TWO

RICKY: I give her a few minutes she come around.

(BLOW *crosses to other side of bed; begins to arrange pillow and sheet around* JOHN ANTHONY'*s body.*)

BLOW: You got the niggers a little while, you got Augie at midnight. You ain't got but a coupla bucks. You ain't got the blow. If the nigger leave you on your feet— maybe he's in a hurry? Hey. Maybe he's in a hurry?—if he leave you standin' up then you tell Augie to take it out in trade. Take you maybe—let's see you gonna be maybe sixty when you pay him off. He'll wait. Hey? Then he goes and tells Mike.

RICKY: I give her a few minutes.

BLOW: Give her a few, that's right, Ricky, give her `til you layin' on the floor holding your guts. I seen it once, a manager he thinks he own the fuckin' bar. They tell him— Hey. You don't own fuckin' nothin'. He deal like he own his own mother ass and they get pissed off. One morning I'm with the bartender he take me into the bar to suck me a quick one you know what I mean? For him it's free. You shoulda seen it, Ricky. (*Pause*) The manager like his head was blown clean fuckin' away. (*Pause*) But it was the manager's punk, some kid he pick up in Florida? (*Pause*) They cut him from his tits to his cock hang him up behind the bar. (*Pause*) So maybe the nigger *don't* cut you. He's a mean cocksucker but he don't kill your ass. Anyway let's don't worry about niggers. It's Mike, man. He think you only lookin' funny at him he tear off your suckin' nose. You and Crank and Mitchell you work outa here like you belong to Mike. Mike think you belong to him he get right away suspicious, think you onna grab. He don't really care what you grab he don't care how much. It's because you reachin' for it. It's when you spread your fingers and lean over—*that's* what give Mike the hots. Just that you want. He hates it that you fuckin' want. *(Pause)* It's like his own face is starin' back at him.

(Pause)

RICKY: It ain't only my ass, bohunk.

BLOW: Is this one reachin', Ricky? Or Augie, you think Augie is reachin'? Augie's a manager. Managers—it's part of the set-up they get a little. Rip time is part of the set-up. Augie's not reachin'—Mike is *givin'* it to him.

RICKY: I wait a few minutes. You shut your fuck, do what I say.

BLOW: You member that little redhead, the hooker hadda cock bigger than he was? Starts at the Haymarket just like you and me. Member him? He start punkin' for some competitor Mike don't fuckin' like. Big fat pig inna limo drives up to G G's like it was his? So Mike ask the redhead a favor. The redhead he spills to the fat pig in the limo. O K. The fat pig he still drivin' up to G G's like there was searchlights at the door. But the kid they fuckin' peel off his lips. They don't kill his ass but you try suckin' cock when you got no lips on your fuckin' face.

RICKY: The niggers kill my ass. Mike kill my ass. So I fuckin' give her a few minutes, Blow. You hear me, Blow? *(Pause. Then he descends to his knees to shout under bed.)* You fuckin' pussy! You actin' like a bitch you pussy like a little bitch!

BLOW: That won't work with him, Ricky.

RICKY: Oh Jesus.

BLOW: It was crazy from the start, Ricky. Roper you suckin' right, Roper *is* pussy. He don't *like* pussy.

RICKY: Oh Jesus.

BLOW: Roper carry these toys like they was his basket. He come here so maybe the *kid* is gonna show cock. But

ACT TWO 59

he can't *act* like pussy. He can't act like pussy Eighth Avenue, he can't act like pussy Sixth. He hopin' the kid will go, Hey. You know with the poppers and shit. Hey. You like it up the ass hey baby hey baby. Roper go, Shut up, kid, real rough like voice down to here. Shut up, kid. Roper is big, but the kid with his pretty face it's the pretty face Roper wants to see over him, bangin' him slappin' him cuttin' him. The kid goes, Hey cunt. Real high, little boy voice. He turns Roper's arm a little, turns his arm a little in the socket. Roper goes, Oh shit, that's my bad arm, kid. Kid goes, Cunt. Cunt. Pussy cunt. Oh baby you pussy cunt feel it up your hole. And there's this pretty little kid wailin' on Roper's ass.

(There is a knocking at the door.)

BLOW: The niggers.

(RICKY rises to his feet, backs towards bathroom door.)

RICKY: I gotta think, Blow. Lean on 'em a little I gotta....

BLOW: Oh shit, Ricky.

RICKY: They're early. Give 'em the money in her purse. Tell 'em to come back maybe an hour.

BLOW: Oh shit, Ricky.

RICKY: Shut your fuck do what I say, Blow! *(He exits into bathroom, closing door.)*

(BLOW stands in silence, staring after RICKY. There is more knocking, only BLOW does not move. There is knocking again. BLOW abruptly crosses to bed and fusses with sheet, musingly fingering a lock of JOHN ANTHONY's hair.)

(There is more knocking. Finally, BLOW moves upstage to door. Breathes deeply. Whips open door. Enter CRANK and MITCHELL, tentatively, speaking in a kind of hush.)

MITCHELL: What the ka-fuck? You don't let shiksas like us stand around in hallways. Bad enough the street door is broke.

CRANK: Where's Ricky?

(BLOW, *relieved, gestures towards bathroom; moves downstage to sit in chair by the bed. He looks into* ROPER's *wallet, which* RICKY *has left on the floor next to the chair.* CRANK *and* MITCHELL *come tentatively downstage.)*

CRANK: *(Continued, in low tones to* BLOW*)* Thinkin' again?

MITCHELL: So where's all the whips and chains?

(CRANK *sits on the bed's right margin.)*

CRANK: Is the shit come? Niggers get here yet?

MITCHELL: The halters, you know? The fist scene? Did she even *notice* the kid is cacked?

CRANK: Ricky he got the money. Right, Blow?

MITCHELL: The *kid* is still here. No shit stains on the *ceiling*. What I wanna know is what happened with Roper?

CRANK: Ricky shoult'na had me promise them niggers fat five. Blow? Shoult'na promise.

MITCHELL: It hadda be such a comedy? Up the peehole. *(Goofing)* What you mean I kill this kid? All I did was pull her teeth with my silver wrenches.

BLOW: Roper's under the bed.

(CRANK *jumps up from bed.)*

CRANK: Motherfuck!

MITCHELL: Blow, you shittin' me? *(He descends to knees; peers under bed.)* Hey. You musta fed her enough dust to fill a pothole. She's under there shakin' like a Pekinese. Hey. Mister Roper. Don't worry. It's just you know like it's just temporary. I know it *feels* like

ACT TWO 61

permanent brain damage. But tomorrow you get up, you walk around, you take a shit, you get bored, you toke up another, you do it all over again only this time it's a kick in the tits. Laugh? You will piss your panties, Mister Roper. *(To* BLOW*)* You get any money offa the bitch?

BLOW: A coupla bucks maybe.

CRANK: A coupla bucks! Hey. Blow. Them niggers is comin' here.

BLOW: And this card you know how to use this card?

MITCHELL: Oh sure niggers take credit cards.

CRANK: So Ricky he's thinkin'? A new operation?

BLOW: Upper East. He work outa one of them services, you know what I mean? Dinners at a French restaurant hunnert dollars a night. Gonna be a *escort.*

MITCHELL: Gonna be a dead man that shvartzer find him.

CRANK: Or Mike?

(Still on his knees, MITCHELL *begins hissing under the bed.)*

MITCHELL: Hey. Mister Roper. You this consultant, right? So give us the word. A coupla black bitches, kinna mean but anyway they got a sense of humor? And a low-level capo he likes to bend back your fingers. Then there's us hookers. If you was us hookers, what would you do? Know what I mean? Like if you had this one corporation won't deliver because of you know mismanagement? And there's this other corporation wantin' more money than was ever around in the first place? They ain't got much muscle but *much* muscle they don't need. But the real problem is the third corporation. *They* got muscle. If the first corporation don't put out, then the second don't come across, and then you see what I mean? The third corporation says, O K, sluts, fuck for blood.

CRANK: Blow? Mike gonna rub glass in our eyes?

MITCHELL: So Mister Roper what do they pay you for?

BLOW: Crank, all this time you and Ricky act like you live here.

MITCHELL: So consult our asses, you bitch!

BLOW: You come, you go Crank. Don't tie up with nobody. Keep it small. Keep it like if somebody ask you, can you hold this shit while he fucks off uptown, you say, Oh man I'm too stoned, could you get me a cab?

CRANK: So he's gonna rub glass in our eyes? Blow?

BLOW: I don't know, Crank. Maybe not. Maybe he don't care so much.

MITCHELL: You fuckin' G M queen you fuckin' Sixth Avenue rage piece! *(He suddenly stands; crosses to bureau.)* I'm puttin out for these numbers since I'm fifteen years old. *(He starts brushing his hair before bureau mirror.)* Fulla shit, every one. You know how they get to the fiftieth floor? The fiftieth floor is just fifty blow jobs piled on toppa each other! A lotta two-bit Jews and three-piece Goyim. *(Stops brushing hair; into mirror.)* I'm scared, Blow.

(Pause)

BLOW: So maybe Mike don't find out everything.

MITCHELL: You knew Mike was gonna find out?

BLOW: I don't know nothin.

MITCHELL: Mike gonna find out, why the ka-fuck you hangin' around?

BLOW: For the kid.

(Pause)

ACT TWO

MITCHELL: For that stinkin' corpse?

BLOW: He was a nice kid—ditn't do nothin.

MITCHELL: That kid, Blow? That kid come here for cock. I see her stick her arm out. She wadn't dreamin about you. She was hot for cock. Any cock up her ass in her mouth.

BLOW: Shut up, Mitchell.

(MITCHELL *begins violently brushing his hair; speaking into mirror.*)

MITCHELL: They look at magazines in Utica, Blow. Come here think it's a magazine, big cocks and hairy chests.

BLOW: Shut the fuck up, Mitchell!

CRANK: Ricky. Maybe Ricky has a new operation?

MITCHELL: *(Ceases brushing; looks hard at* BLOW*)* You shakin' too, Blow. How much of that shit you suck up?

BLOW: Skin like. All over his body is like the skin on your fuckin' behind.

MITCHELL: *(Rolling his eyes to ceiling)* This the weird room. This the number one weird room onna Deuce.

(*There is rasping of the lock; enter* AUGIE *through entrance door.*)

AUGIE: Jeez. Where the fuck is Roper you cunts?

MITCHELL: You a little early ain't you early, Augie?

AUGIE: You end up dead I come at midnight, bitch. Where's Roper?

MITCHELL: Under the bed?

(*Pause*)

AUGIE: *(Toneless)* Under the fuckin' bed.

MITCHELL: He crawls under the bed what can we do?

AUGIE: *Drag him outa there!*

(Immediately CRANK *and* MITCHELL *work at pulling* ROPER *from beneath the bed.)*

AUGIE: *(To* BLOW.*)* Where's greaseball?

BLOW: Inna toilet. Niggers be here real soon. You wanna see if they take this card?

AUGIE: Fuckin' jeez. Where you get that?

BLOW: In her wallet. Ricky says you can talk to machines with it.

AUGIE: Give me the fuckin' wallet.

*(*BLOW *hands over card and wallet to* AUGIE.*)*

BLOW: We flash that card at them maybe everything happen like Ricky say.

AUGIE: Niggers ain't runnin this deal no more, so fuck off with the cutes, Blow. *(He crosses to bathroom door, loudly.)* Mike wanna know Ricky come and see him.

(The bathroom door opens. Enter RICKY *with a tourniquet around his arm, holding a syringe.)*

AUGIE: What you doin there, greaseball?

RICKY: Just a taste—so what?

AUGIE: A that same shit offa Blow?

RICKY: Just a taste I said! Now what you fuck?

AUGIE: Mike wants you should come and see him, Ricky.

(Pause)

RICKY: *(Gesturing with "fit")* You a pussy wipe, Augie.

AUGIE: You should be sayin' this to me.

RICKY: You pussied out, Augie, you go to Mike!

AUGIE: To me he says this.

ACT TWO

RICKY: We coulda got outa here, Augie! This was in the pocket.

AUGIE: Pussy she calls me. That hurts, asshole.

RICKY: *(Straight into* AUGIE's *face.)* Mike is runnin' this deal? He give you better terms?

BLOW: Hey. Mitchell. I am so fuckin' surprised.

MITCHELL: *(While pulling at* ROPER.*)* And we are so fuckin' crippled.

AUGIE: *(Casually looking away from* RICKY; *to the room.)* Mike ain't gonna hurt nobody.

RICKY: *(Toneless)* Ain't gonna hurt nobody.

AUGIE: I ain't hurt so why he hurt you?

RICKY: You fuckin', you fuckin', you fuckin' tell Mike.

AUGIE: No, I ditn't.

(He crosses to MITCHELL *and* CRANK, *who have succeeded in pulling* ROPER *from under bed.* ROPER *is curled in a ball with arms crossed over chest and eyes shut.)*

AUGIE: Hey. Mister Roper. You know me, it's Augie.

ROPER: Augie?

RICKY: So who tell Mike, Augie?

AUGIE: Hey. Mister Roper. Tits up.

RICKY: Who tell Mike I ask you a fuckin' question!

(Pause. AUGIE *looks at* RICKY, *glances here and there about the room, and then settles his gaze on* BLOW.*)*

AUGIE: So who tell Mike, Blow?

*(*BLOW *does not respond.)*

AUGIE: I wonner who rip the panties off this fuckin' operation? I wonner who call and say, Hey. Mike. Some kinna weird up there those stupid fags. Buncha

65

Gucci Dior coke buncha nigger lowlifes messin' your room. I wonner who do that, Blow?

BLOW: *(Rising and turning away)* I don't work for you, Augie.

AUGIE: *(Rising and crossing to* BLOW; *spinning him around)* Oh yeah right. You come you go you suck you fuck. Don't belong to nobody I heard that shit. Now you answer me, Blow.

RICKY: Blow?

AUGIE: Mike lissen to you you bohunk you cocksuck. And I gotta dance up there and go, Oh shit, I am shocked up my clitteris. Then I gotta say I will find out these fags what they fuckin' doin over there. Twice I gotta dance for Mike. Then I gotta say, Fuckin' jeez, there's not only these niggers and this coke there's this dead fetus. And Mike, what you think Mike say, Blow?

(BLOW *does not respond. He is trying to look away, but* AUGIE *keeps ducking his face under* BLOW's *fugitive gaze.)*

AUGIE: He go, Oh? *(Pause)* Oh yeah? *(Pause)* Now why you do that, Blow?

(BLOW *turns away without responding.)*

RICKY: You fuckin' answer him, bohunk!

BLOW: Ricky try and sell the kid.

(Pause)

(RICKY *crosses to* BLOW *and stares at his back. Then he slowly turns and approaches bed. Looks at body)*

RICKY: You fetus? You feature this? Blow fuck, he fuck my deal for you, you little shit. He fuckin', he fuckin'....

MITCHELL: Jesus, Blow.

(RICKY *turns from bed and crosses to* BLOW *again and stares at his back as before.* RICKY *raises "fit" menacingly, like a*

ACT TWO

shiv, then despairingly drops hand. He turns from BLOW, *slowly shaking his head, and crosses to bathroom.)*

AUGIE: Mike thinks maybe you should come and see him, Ricky. He knows you was gonna tell him, but he wants to make sure you unnerstan' the procedures. Knows you wadn't gonna finalize without him. Says to tell you, he admires your fuckin' initiative, Ricky.

(RICKY *enters bathroom soundlessly, carefully closing the door behind him.)*

MITCHELL: Ka-fuck.

(AUGIE *crosses to* BLOW.)

AUGIE: So you don't work for me, right, Blow?

(BLOW *is staring at the body; he does not lift his eyes.)*

BLOW: That's right, Augie.

AUGIE: "That's right, Augie." You fucking right I'm right. The one you workin' for now is Mike.

BLOW: I come I go, Augie.

AUGIE: "I come I go, Augie." You fuckin' right. When Mike say come, you come, when he say go, you go. He says to me I gotta keep a eye on you, Blow. He knows it was your dirt cacked the kid, Blow.

BLOW: You tell him that, Augie?

AUGIE: And he wants your twat outa here down the Village, Blow.

(Pause)

BLOW: I come I go, Augie.

AUGIE: And when you get more dirt to peddle it comes through this operation. Hey? And when you stick your big bohunk cock up somebody's hole we tell you who's hole, how deep and when to fuckin' shoot. Got that, Blow?

(Pause)

BLOW: *(Almost a whisper)* So fuckin' what?

AUGIE: "So fuckin' what?" So Mike has got control, that's fuckin' what. Control. The one you workin' for now is Mike. *(He crosses to stand over ROPER.)* Hey. Mister Roper, Mike wants I should take you home.

ROPER: Augie?

AUGIE: Hey. You get kinna fucked up? Fuckin' happens, Mister Roper, know what I mean?

ROPER: Augie?

MITCHELL: So what about the niggers?

AUGIE: Cops take care of them.

MITCHELL: The what, Augie?

AUGIE: *(Checking watch)* You tell Mike those black mothers come here at ten, right, Blow? That don't give us much time, bitches.

CRANK: You mean like police and shit?

AUGIE: Niggers are holdin'. They get here about ten minutes after the Midtown Precinct.

MITCHELL: Augie. I am not dressed for the Midtown Precinct.

AUGIE: Mike got control. I gotta say that. Can you see the big write-up inna *Daily News*? "White Kid Cacked by Dope and Niggers." *(Pause)* What I'm sayin' is the niggers take the heat for the fetus.

(Pause, as the others stare)

AUGIE: Fuckin' Christ. I mean, Mike has got his fingers up product. Cops look good. They take pictures. All them bozos out in Queens eat it up.

CRANK: So the niggers is gonna pay? Augie?

ACT TWO 69

AUGIE: Cops eat some of that coke, we stretch the rest. It's under control. Blow, you hang out the Village for a while. *(Looks hard at* BLOW*)* Like Mike wants.

BLOW: *(Dazed; emotionless)* Cops take care of him, Augie. Send his body home.

AUGIE: *(Toneless)* Send his body home.

BLOW: *(Same)* Mike ain't gonna put the kid in the river. Cops send his body home.

AUGIE: Tie a pink ribbon on his weewee send him right home, Blow. Fuckin' jeez. You all hang out the Village. 'Cept Ricky. Hey. Mister Roper. You wanna try standin' up? That's right.

(AUGIE *helps* ROPER *into a chair.*)

CRANK: Augie? He ain't gonna rub glass in our eyes?

(AUGIE *glowers at* CRANK.)

AUGIE: Shut your cocksuck.

ROPER: He's not really dead, Augie. He's not really, is he?

AUGIE: Of course not, Mister Roper.

ROPER: A large ugly joke.

AUGIE: A bozo scene—it ain't real.

ROPER: Not real. Of course not. Augie?

CRANK: Blow. He don't break our fingers?

AUGIE: Come on, Mister Roper. This your briefcase, right? *(Picks up briefcase after snapping it shut.)* We get a cab, go to your place, you get inna hot tub. Mike he send you his compliments, says he will take care of everything.

(*He helps* ROPER *towards the entrance door. To the others*)

AUGIE: You queens got maybe twenny minutes. I don't wanna see your assholes these facilities. Tell Ricky I see him the Haymarket. We go see Mike.

(Exits with ROPER *through entrance door)*

CRANK: Mitchell?

MITCHELL: What the fuck I stash in this pit? *(He crosses to bureau, rummages.)*

CRANK: Mitchell? Our foots ain't gonna be in Brooklyn our elbows in Jersey?

*(*MITCHELL *is stuffing oddments from bureau into purse.)*

MITCHELL: Our asses in the Village that's all I know. Only, you never see that kid.

CRANK: I never see her.

MITCHELL: You did not geeze her ass.

CRANK: Would I shoot up a minor?

*(*BLOW *stares at bathroom door.)*

BLOW: Ricky? *(Pause)* Ricky hey. *(He crosses to bathroom door.)*

MITCHELL: *(To* CRANK*)* You was workin', where was you workin' last night?

CRANK: The Haymarket?

MITCHELL: Who saw you?

CRANK: The bartender?

*(*BLOW *opens bathroom door, looks inside. Abruptly he closes bathroom door; stares at it.)*

MITCHELL: *(Still rummaging.)* Yesterday I was so suckin' relieve I miss the gang bang at Bryant Park? Now I wish they'd a ka-fucking arrested me. Blow, you hear they got that Black Maria now drive right inna park? They drag you in there kick the shit outa you hand you a summons. One J and they drag you in there. Two

ACT TWO

pounds a scag you can diddle a cop you can fuckin' diddle the schmucky mayor. But one loose J they drag you in there and rip out your pussy. Yesterday I wish they woulda.

CRANK: *(To* MITCHELL*)* Christopher Street? How we gonna deal for shit on Christopher? That's sissy that's poopie.

MITCHELL: *(Pausing)* Blow?

(BLOW *turns and crosses slowly to bed. He begins to straighten sheet around body. Finds T-shirt. Stares at it)*

MITCHELL: Blow?

(BLOW *stuffs T-shirt in his back pocket. Looks at body)*

BLOW: *(Still looking at body; to* MITCHELL*)* Don't worry about Ricky no more.

(Pause)

MITCHELL: Ka-fuck.

(BLOW *crosses to entrance door and wordlessly exits.)*

MITCHELL: Hey. Blow. See you downtown? *(Pause)* Come on, Crank, let's get our titties in gear. You leave anything this apartment?

CRANK: What do Blow mean don't worry about Ricky?

MITCHELL: What Blow means is don't worry about Ricky. Anybody ask, he's asleep on the toilet. Like today ditn't happen. Hey. Crank. Where is Ricky?

CRANK: Asleep on the toilet, last night I leave him passed out on the toilet.

MITCHELL: Where?

CRANK: Asleep on the toilet?

(MITCHELL *turns from bureau, looks about room. Crosses to bed; switches sheet away, exposing* JOHN ANTHONY's *naked body.)*

MITCHELL: Give those undercover cunts a thrill. Where, Crank?

CRANK: On the toilet?

MITCHELL: Where the fuck was you all day?

CRANK: Fifty-third and Third.

MITCHELL: Where?

CRANK: A Toyota a Datsun and a Buick convertible?

MITCHELL: Who inna Buick convertible would pick you up?

CRANK: A Mazda?

(Exit MITCHELL *and* CRANK *through entrance door. Their voices can still be heard offstage.)*

MITCHELL: Where's Ricky?

CRANK: Asleep on the toilet, Mitchell.

MITCHELL: Where?

CRANK: The cocksuckin' toilet!

(Lights up on the body)

(Slow curtain)

END OF PLAY

GLOSSARY

The idiom employed in the play is special to the New York streets or, in some instances, an outright invention of the author. A glossary to the slang and local references most used is here provided.

"blow": Cocaine

"crank": Low-grade methedrine *(speed)*

"to cack": To die; East Coast slang for giving up the ghost, "cacking", or vomiting up the spirit

"fetus": A very young, innocent child. In other words, a mere unformed baby

"Forty-deuce" specifically refers to Forty-second Street, but is generic for the entire Times Square area, the world's most vital wholesale/retail center for the sex and drug industries

"fuck": The most serviceable word on the New York streets, employed as noun, verb, or adjective. It is used, of course, in its traditional Anglo-Saxon sense, but also as a general expletive; to indicate absolute nullity; to replace milder four-letter words; etc. The phrase used by RICKY—"What you fuck?"—is an uninflected challenge meaning "Where do you get off?/Who do you think you are?"

"to geeze": To inject drugs intravenously

"guinea/greaser": Ethnic slurs; a person of Italian extraction

Local References:

The Haymarket: An Eighth Avenue bar famed in the Times Square area, frequented by youthful male hustlers, their johns and pimps.

Tompkins Square: BLOW's home territory, on the Lower East Side of Manhattan, where Ukrainians have long been in conflict with blacks and Puerto Ricans.

East New York: Where RICKY and CRANK hail from, a tough, generally white section of Brooklyn.

Boro Park: In Queens, a Hasidic area, rigidly straight and straitlaced; a Jewish queen's nightmare.

Port Authority: The vast Manhattan bus terminal through which most runaways are likely to pass.

Sixth Avenue: Shorthand for the Avenue of the Americas, in midtown Manhattan; corporate heart of the nation.

Dixie Hotel: Once famous, now defunct hotel where more sedate johns entertained ladies and boys.

Bryant Park: Attached to the Public Library on Forty-second Street, on and off a thriving drug retail market.

www.ingramcontent.com/pod-product-compliance
Lightning Source LLC
Chambersburg PA
CBHW060215050426
42446CB00013B/3074